Library of
Davidson College

Rufus Festus Avienus

ORA MARITIMA

*(Description of the Seacoast
from Brittany to Marseilles [Massilia])*

Rufus Festus Avienus

ORA MARITIMA

A
DESCRIPTION OF THE SEACOAST
FROM BRITTANY TO
MARSEILLES [MASSILIA]

LATIN TEXT
WITH FACING ENGLISH TRANSLATION,
COMMENTARY, NOTES, INDICES AND
FACSIMILE OF THE *EDITIO PRINCEPS*

By

J. P. MURPHY, S.J.

ARES PUBLISHERS INC.
CHICAGO, ILLINOIS MCMLXXVII

Publication of this book has been made possible by a grant from the John and Helen Condon Fund.

Copyright 1977
ARES PUBLISHERS INC.
CHICAGO, ILLINOIS
Printed in the United States of America
International Standard Book Number:
0-89005-175-5

A Prefatory Note on the Two Previous Reference Editions of Avienus' *Ora Maritima*

A. Schulten's Edition

Anyone who works in Avienus owes very much to Adolph Schulten. I acknowledge my debt forthwith. Although his views, most notably on the location of Tartessus, are sometimes disputed, nonetheless his lifetime of work in Spanish antiquity commands respect and attention for his views. In 1922 he published in Latin his *Avieno: Ora Martima (Fontes Hispaniae Antiquae I)*. Twenty-three years later in 1955, a second edition appeared. The introduction and commentary are written in Spanish, and Jos6. Rius y Serra did a Spanish translation of the poem. Most of what appears in this present commentary derives from that edition of Schulten's. Unless otherwise noted, his views referred to in the commentary are taken from that work.

Avienus' contribution to ancient geography consists, of course, in his preserving for us fragments of a much earlier geographical work. The author of this geographical work was a Massiliote who produced *a Periplus,* describing the shore from Tartessus to Massilia. The author included reports he had heard from the Tartessians on the northern and western shores of the Ocean up to Brittany. The Tartessians also gave to the Massiliotes reports on Ireland and Great Britain, which they had received from the Oestrymnici, the then natives of Brittany. As to how ancient this Massiliote author is, Schulten argued for *circa* 520 B.C. Thus the *Periplus* would preceed Hecataeus and be on of the first works in Greek prose. Rhys Carpenter (*Beyond the Pillars of Hercules,* pp. 200-01) argued that Avienus' source, either directly or indirectly, was Pythias of Massilia. Thus Carpenter dated the *Periplus* to the fourth century. Schulten would need an earlier writer and his suggestion is Euthymenes. Euthymenes is a sixth century B.C. author who described the western Ocean.

The next level to be found in Avienus is that of the interpolator. Schulten feels he is a Greek author who wrote in the first century B.C.

a *Periplus* of the Mediterranean Sea This author used the ancient Massiliote *Periplus* together with the eleven authors of the sixth and fifth centuries B.C. who are cited as authorities in lines 32-50 of Avienus' *Ora Matitima*. This use, however, of other authors was most likely not direct, but through an intermediary writer such as Ephorus. The interpolator made additions of his own.

The final level is Avienus' Latin translation made about 400 A.D. There are obvious additions that Avienus himself wrote such as the dedication to Probus (lines 1-31) or the reference to Juba's duumvirate Oines 270-83).

To sum up, then, the method of the *Ora Matitima's* composition, I cite Schulten's summary statement (p. 54):

> El periplo marsellés del año hacia 500 a. C redactado en prosa fué puesto hacia 100 a. C. en versos trimetros por un maestro griego. Este maestro griego añadió al periplo interpolaciones. Estas interpolaciones, en parte, estan sacadas de Eforo, en parte son del mismo maestro. Tal obra del maestro griego fué traducida al latin por Avieno hacia 400 p. C. añadiendo interpolaciones propias en parte doctas en parte ermneas.

A. Berthelot's Edition

Besides Schulten's the most significant work done on Avienus' *Ora Maritima* in this century is that of A. Berthelot. That edition was published in 1934 at Paris by Honore Champion (*Librairie Ancienne*) under the title: *Festus Avienus: Ora Maritima. Edition annotee, precedee d'une Introduction et accompagnée d'un Commentaire.* In addition to the Introduction and Commentary, Berthelot has also given a French translation of the poem except for the first 31 lines, and has added two notes, one on the indications of distances, the other on the dates of the materials in the *Ora Maritima*. He also summarizes his positions in a Conclusion, and gives a good index.

Upon its appearance, Berthelot's edition met with favorable comment. Thus, for example, E. H. Warmington wrote in a review, "There can be little doubt that in most places where Prof. Berthelot disagrees with the work of previous scholars on Avienus he is right" (*JRS* 27 [1937], p. 308). it is to be regretted, therefore, that Schutten virtually ignored Berthelot's edition in his own second edition of Avienus' *Ora Maritima* in 1955. On the one page on which he explicitly mentions the French edition, Schulten dismissed Berthelot's correction of the *editio princeps'* reading *pernix lucis* to *pernis Lusis* as an error that only an *ingeniero* and not a *filologo* would make. Schulten does grant, however, that Berthelot's commentary has value for the coast of Provence, which the Frenchman knew well. The neglect of Berthelot by Schulten may have been prompted by Berthelot's polemics when he referred to Mallenhofrs and Schulten's theories as *"laborieuses fictions,"* a *roman,"* and a *"château de cartes."* Berthelot however, does see value in Schulten's careful, line-by-line commentary on the text even if he feels he must depart from many of Schulten's positions (*"je prends souvent le contrepied,"* p. 17).

As to the text of Avienus' *Ora Maritima,* Berthelot supplies one, mainly for the user of the commentary. It is a very conservative text, which, for the most part, follows Holder's edition. For a full list of variants and corrections, Berthelot refers the reader to Holder. Upon occasion Berthelot returns to Victor Pisanus' *editio princeps* for a reading. He also found valuable readings in Ortellius' manuscript version. The corrections of Pithou, Hudson, and Wernsdorf are given selectively, now in the text, now in the notes. Berthelot also retained fourth century A.D. spellings (e.g. *nanque* for *namque, negociandi* for *negotiandi*). These factors combine to made the text unattractive and difficult to read. Schulten's and even Holder's texts are superior. There one does not meet such atrocious lines as "*Tibi haud sit ullo, orestis et dur reor*" (line 13) or "*Salyes atroces, oppidum priscum ra Mastrabalae*" (line 701).

Berthelot outlines the *Ora Maritima* as follows:
Preamble: lines 1-79
First Part: Atlantic Shore and Columns of Hercules:
    lines 80-415
  A. lines 80-145: Atlantic Shore (to Spain)
  B. lines 146-204: Atlantic Shore of Spain
  C. lines 205-415: Region of the Columns

Second Part: From Columns to Marseilles: lines 416-703
  A. lines 416-557: Mediterranean Shore to the Pyrenees
  B. lines 558-703: From the Pyrenees to Marseilles

In the commentary Berthelot divides the second part (lines 416-703) into five, not two, subdivisions, undoubtedly for ease of presentation. Before the commentary on each section, Berthelot gives a French translation of the text under consideration.

The most fundamental difference between Berthelot and Schulten is that the former rejects the latter's theory of three layers in the text (that is, 1) a VI century B.C. Massiliot *Periplus*: 2) a Greek interpolator of the first century B.C.; 3) Avienus). Rather, Berthelot proposes that Avienus did exactly what he said he did, namely, he garnered from many ancient authorities notices on the Spanish coast and beyond. Avienus followed the archaizing trend of his age and thus felt the older the material, the better. He was writing for the antiquarian and scholar in his study, not for the traveller in need of a good guide-book. Berthelot assigns an ancient date (VI-IV century B.C.) for much of the material in Avienus, but does not do justice to the antiquity of much of the text. The appearance of so many place and tribal names not otherwise attested requires explanation. Further, in many places, Berthelot denies that the source was a *periplus* at all, and notices on the interior and its tribes do present a problem for Schulten's hypothesis of a VI century B.C. Massiliot *Periplus* as the ancient document underlying Avienus' poem.

The next most notable difference in the two commentaries is that Berthelot denies the Massiliot origin of the older document. In addition to materials that seem foreign to a *periplus,* his main grounds for this are that the description of Massilia in lines 704-712 is very poor and could not have been written by a native of that city. He asks where is the swamp (*stagnum* again) that laps (*lambit,* Berthelot's reading) or surrounds (*ambit,* Schulten's reading) the town. Further there are not traces of any man-made works that have changed the natural site although this is what the poem explicitly states was done: *Labos et olim conditorum diligens/Forman locorum et arua naturalia/Evicit arte* (lines 710-12). Hence Berthelot concludes, "*Il est inconcevable que des auteurs fort sérieux aient juge cette description de Marseille exact et impliquant l'origine massaliote de son auteur*" (p. 130).

As to the tribes and peoples mentioned in Avienus, Berthelot considers the Oestrymnians to be a Celtic people, who moved by sea to Brittany and the British Isles. From there they migrated to Jutland, the Danish peninsula. Thus Berthelot holds that lines 129-145 of the *Ora Maritima* recall historical events that go as far back as the XII or XI century B.C. Schulten thought that the Oestrymnians were Ligurians.

With regard to the Ligurians, Berthelot rejects the correction *Ligus* in line 196 and denies the presence of Ligurians in the Iberian peninsula. Most scholars would agree with Berthelot on this point. He also suggested a correction of line 284's *Ligustino* to *Libustino*, meaning Libyan. He pointed out that later (lines 417) Avienus uses *Libystide* with this meaning. At any rate there is no other shred of evidence for locating the Ligurians at the mouth of the Baetis.

The valley of the Baetis brings to mind the Tartessians. This people Berthelot held to be of Libyan or Moorish origin, rather than from Asia Minor as Schulten had suggested. Berthelot considers the Phoenician presence at Gades as a commercial enclave, rather than as a political hegemony. Even after the Carthaginians conquered the area, the Tartessians played the intermediary in the tin trade.

As for the Iberians, Berthelot rejected an African origin for them and held that the evidence of lines 248-53 of the *Ora Maritima* is not strong enough to bear such an interpretation. In those verses, Berthelot felt that Avienus was trying to stun the reader, and has been misled by an accidental resemblance of two geographical names (*Hiberus*).

Berthelot's longest disquisition on any one point contradicts Schulten and other "philologists" concerning Mt. Clape's having once been an island (pp. 114-21 of his commentary). From geology and the analysis of various texts and maps, Berthelot concluded that the shore line has undergone very little change since antiquity.

That Berthelot has made good contributions to the study of Avienus is beyond question. It is unfortunate that the polemics seemed to have hampered, or rather blocked, communications with Schulten. However, both scholars are needed for the study of Avienus' text and of ancient geography in general. As the work of archaeology in Spain progresses, more light will be thrown on the obviously ancient materials in Avienus, and the conflicts in these two scholars' views may be resolved.

Chronological List of Editions of Avienus' *Ora Maritima*

1488: Victor Pisanus. Venice. (Reproduced in this edition pp. 101-119).
1590: Peter Pithou. In *Epigrammata et poematia vetera*. Paris.
1634: Peter Melian. In *Ruffi Festi Avieni v. c. Hispani Opera quae extant*. Madrid.
1712: John Hudson. In vol. 4 of *Geographiae vetetis scriptores graeci*. Oxford.
1713: Michael Maittaire. In vol. 2 of *Opera et fragmenta veterum poetarum Latinorum Profanorum & Ecclesiasticorum*. London.
1717: ____. *In Dionysii orbis descriptio, cum Eustathii commentariis et Anonymi paraphrasi graeca. Accedunt Antiquae Versiones Prisciani & R. Festi Avieni*. Oxford.
1737: Jean Astruc. In *Mémoires pour l'histoire naturelle de Languedoc*. (Avienus' description of the coast of Narbonese Gaul) Paris.
1766: *Collectio Pisaurensis*. In vol. 4. Pesaro.
1789: Sainte Croix. In *Journal des Savants*.
1792: John Wernsdorf. In vol. 5 of *Poetae latini minores*. Helmstadt.
1809: ____. *In Collection de géographes latins*. Strasbourg.
1825: N. E. Lemaire. In *Bibliotheca classica Latina*. Paris.
1835: Miguel Cortés y López. In *Diccionario geográphico*. Madrid.
1842: C. Panckoucke. In *Seconde série de la Bibliothèque latine-française traductions nouvelles des auteurs latins avec le texte en regard depuis Adrien jusqu'a Grégoire de Tours*. Paris.
1848: J. A. Giles. Reprint of Wernsdorf. London.
1887: Alfred Holder. Innsbruck.
1906: *Revue des études anciennes* XVIII, no. 4. (Facsimile of the *editio princeps'* passage on Languedoc).
1909: Antonio Blázques. In *El Periplo de Himilco*. Madrid.
1922: Adolph Schulten. Vol. I *in Fontes Hispaniae Antiquae*. Berlin.
1934: A. Berthelot. Paris.
1955: Adolph Schulten. 2nd edition. Barcelona.
1965: Alfred Holder. Reprint of 1887 edition. Hildesheim.
1968: Dietrich Stichtenoth. Darmstadt.

CONTENTS

A Prefatory Note on the Two Previous
    Reference Editions of Avienus' *Ora Maritima*.......... v
        A. Schulten's Edition........................ v
        A. Berthelot's Edition....................... vi
Chronological List of Editions of
    Avienus' *Ora Maritima*...................... x
Contents... xi
List of Maps... xii

RVFI FESTI AVIENI, *Ora Maritima*
    Sigla.. 1
Latin text... 2
English Translation.................................. 3
Commentary.. 49
Select Bibliography.................................. 81
Index: Geographical Sites in Avienus'
    Ora Maritima and their Present Names............. 83
Index of Proper Names................................ 89
Appendix... 99
    The *Editio Princeps* of Avienus' *Ora Maritima*....... 100
Facsimile pages............................... 101-119

List of Maps

1. Western Europe according to Avienus
   (after Berthelot, p. 56) 74

2. Western Europe according to Strabo
   (after Berthelot, p. 56a) 75

3. Western Europe according to Agrippa
   (after Berthelot, p. 56b) 76

4. The Iberian Peninsula according to Agrippa
   (after Berthelot, p. 57) 77

5. The Iberian Peninsula according to Avienus
   (Berthelot, p. 64) 78

6. The Iberian Peninsula according to Avienus
   (Schulten) 79

Sigla.

litteris rectis	Periplus
litteris rectis minoribus	interpolationes antiquiores haustae ex Ephoro (?)
litteris cursivis	Avieni magistrive Graeci additamenta
puncto infra posito (a̭)	litterae emendatae
( )	litterae suppletae
[ ]	litterae delendae

Quaesisse temet saepe cogitans, Probe,
animo atque sensu, Taurici ponti situs
capi ut valeret his probabili fide
quos distinerent spatia terrarum extima,
5 *subi libenter id laboris, ut tibi*
desideratum carmine hoc claresceret.
fas non putavi quippe, prolixa die
non, subiacere sensui formam tuo
regionis eius quam vetustis paginis
10 *et qua(m) per omnem spiritus nostri diem*
secretiore lectione acceperam.
alii invidere namque, quod dispendio
tibi haud sit ullo, agretis et dur(i) reor.
his addo et illud, liberum temet loco
15 *mihi esse[t] amor(e) sanguinisque vinculo.*
neque sat sit istud, ni sciam te litteras
hiantibusque, faucibus veterum abdita
hausisse semper, esse patuli pectoris,
sensu capacem, talium iugem sitim
20 *tuo esse cordi et esse te. prae ceteris*
memorem intimati cur inefficaciter
secreta rerum in non tenacem effunderem?
in non sequacem quis profunda ogganniat?
multa ergo, multa computere me, Probe,

Apparatum criticum composuit Alfr. Klotz. O emendationes Ortelianae (cf. Proleg.). Emendationes sine auctoris nomine sunt Pithoei.

RVFI FESTI DESCRIPTIO ORBIS TERRAE EXPLICIT. INCIPIT ORAE MARITIMAE LIBER PRIMVS FELIX.

2 situs *Hudson*: sinus 4 distinerent *Heinisius*: distenerent 5 Subi: subii *Pithou* 13 orestis 14 loco O: *locum* 15 esse amore O: esset amor 16 mice 17 veetrum *Barth*: vestarum *Wernsdrof*.

Thinking, Probus, that you have often asked to be able to grasp with heart and mind the site of the Tauric sea with a reliable assurance even for those whom the most distant ends of the earth separate from it, I have gladly undertaken this work in order that the object of your desire be clarified in this poem **(6)**. Indeed, I did not think it right that at a mature age you do not have before you the shape of that region which I had drawn from old pages and which through every day of my intellectual life I had received from a deeper reading **(11)**. For to begrudge another that which costs you scarcely anything I consider to be the, mark of a bumpkin and boor. To these considerations I add this one too, that you stand for me in the place of a child in love and bond of blood **(15)**. Nor would that be enough if I did not know that you have always drunk in with eagerness literature and the recondite writings of the ancients. You are open-minded, intellectually capable, and have a constant thirst in your heart for such matters. Beyond others you are mindful of inner knowledge **(21)**. Why would I, to no effect, pour out to an incapable person the secrets of things? Who would bark out deep things to one who does not follow? Many things, therefore, Probus, many things compel me to fulfill your earnest

---

Translator's Note: Avienus' *Ora Maritima* has never been completely translated into English. Rhys Carpenter has translated lines 83-141, 267-74, 380-88, 406-14 in *Beyond the Pillars of Hercules* (p. 201-204) and lines 449-63 in *The Greeks in Spain* (p. 52). He successfully imitates the tone of Avienus' verse. It is to be regretted that Carpenter never translated the whole or wrote a full commentary.

The present translation will be a literal prose one.

25	*efflagitatam rem tibi ut persolverem.* *quin et parent(is) credidi officium fore,* *desideratum si tibi locupletius* *profusiusque Musa promeret mea.* *dare expetitum quippe non parci viri est,*
30	*augere porro muneris summa(m) novo* *mentis benignae satque liberatis est.* *Interrogasti, si tenes, Maeotici* *situs qui(s) esset aequoris. Sallustium* *noram id dedisse, dicta et eius omnibus*
35	*praeiudicatae au(c)toritatis ducier* *non abnuebam. ad eius igitur, inclytam,* *descriptionem, qua locorum formulam* *imaginemque expressor efficax stili* *et veritatis paene in optutus dedit*
40	*lepore[m] linguae, multa rerum iunximus* *ex plurimorum, sumpta co(m)mentariis.* *Hecataeus istic quippe erit Milesius* *Hellanicusque Lesbius, Phileus quoque* *Atheniensis, Caryandaeus Scylax,*
45	*Pausimachus inde, prisca quem genuit Samos,* *quin et Damastus nobili natus Sig[n]e.* *Rhodo[n]que Bacoris ortus, Euctemon quoque* *populari(s) urbis Atticae, Siculus Cleon,* *Herodotus ipse Thurius, tum qui decus*
50	*magnum loquendi est, Atticus Thucydides.* *Hic porro habebis, pars mei cordis Probe,* *quicquid per aequor insularum attollitur* *—per aequor illud scilicet, quod post cava* *hiantis orbis a freto Tartes(s)io*
55	*Atlanticisque fluctibus procul si[c]tam* *in usque glaebam proruit nostrum mare—*

---

27 Desidaratum 29 pare 30 novo *Wernsdorf*: novi 40 viximus 42 Haec ad eus mille suis 44 Caryandaeus *Heinsius*: cariae ditus 45 inde *Heinsius*: ille 49 Thurius O: thyrius 56 proruit: porrigit *Wernsdorf*.

request **(25)**. Still more, I have believed it would also be a duty of a parent if my Muse were to relate what you desire more richly and abundantly. For to give what is asked for is a mark of a generous man, but to increase the total gift with something new is a mark of a kind and noble mind **(31)***

You have asked, if you recall, what the site of the Maeotic sea is. I knew that Sallust has given this and I was not going to deny that his words are judged by all to be of preeminent authority **(35)**. Therefore we have joined many things taken from the commentaries of several authors to his famous description in which that effective and truthful stylist has almost perfectly and with charm presented the shape and image of the areas **(40)**. For Hecataeus of Miletus will be present here for you, and Hellanicus of Lesbos, Phileus+ of Athens too, Scylax of Caryanda, and then Pausimachus to whom old Samos gave birth **(45)**. Then too there will be Damastus+ born at famous Sige, and Bacoris from Rhodes, Euctemon too of the democratic city of Athens, Cleon of Sicily, Herodotus himself of Thurii, and then the great glory of eloquence, Attic Thucydides **(50)**.

Here indeed, Probus, part of my heart, you will have whatever islands rise up in the deep—that deep, that is, in which our sea after the recesses of the gaping world from the Tartessian sea and Atlantic waves extends to a far distant land **(56)**. You will also have the curved bays resound with the harsh north wind, but re-

---

*   With line 31 the address to Probus is complete. By way of introduction, Avienus goes on to list his sources (lines 32-50) and then to sketch the scope of his work (lines 51-79).

+   Avienus uses latinized forms of many Greek words. Here the forms of the words should be Phileas and Damastes. However, in the translation, I shall use Avienus' spellings in order to reflect more faithfully what he wrote.

        sinus(que) curvos atque prominentia,
        –ut se supino porrigat litus situ,
        ut longe in undas inserant sese iuga–
60   celsaeque ut urbes alluantur aequore,
        quis ortus amnis maximo(s) effuderit,
        ut prona ponti gurgitem intrant flumina
        ut ipsa[e] rursum saepe cingant insulas
        sinuen que late ut ut tuta portus bra(c)chia,
65   ut explicentur stagna, ceu iaceant lacus,
        scruposum, ut alti verticem montes levent
        stringatque nemora ut unda cana gurgitis.
        laboris autem terminus nostri hic erit,
        Scythicum ut profundum et aequor Euxini sali
70   et siquae in illo marmore insulae tument,
        edisserantur. reliqua porro scripta sunt
        nobis in illo plenius volumine,
        quod de orbis oris partibusque fecimus.
        ut aperta vero tibimet intimatio
75   sudoris huius et laboris sit mei
        narratione(m) opusculi paulo altius
        exordiemur. tu per intimum iecur
        prolata conde, namque fulcit haec fides
        petita longe et eruta ex au(c)toribus.
80   Terrae patentis orbis effus[a]e iace[n]t
        orbique rursus unda circumfunditur.
        sed qua profundum semet insinuat salum
        Oceano ab usque, ut gurges hic nostri maris
        longe explicetur, est Atlanticus sinus.
85   hic Gadir urbs est, dicta Tartessus prius,
        hic sunt columnae pertinacis Herculis
        Abila atque Calpe, (haec) laeva dicti caespitis,
        Libyae propinqu(a) est Abi(l)a. duro perstrepunt

---

    57 *add. Wernsdorf* 64 tute 65 et ut *Heinsius:* ceu 77 per *Hudson ex* 80 *del. Scriverius* 87 *add. Ulitius* 88 propinqua est Abila *Ulitius*: propinque stalia

ceding curve or as the ridges extend themselves far into the waves **(59)**. You will have the great cities that are washed by the sea and what sources pour forth the greatest rivers as the rushing waters enter the swirl of the deep. You will have here information on the islands that the rivers often embrace and the ports that the safe arms of land widely encompass **(64)**. You will read how the lagoons extend, the lakes lie, and how the high mountains raise their rocky heads and how the white wave of the swell touches the forests. This will be the limit of our labor that there be recounted the Scythian deep and sea of Euxine salt water and any islands that rise up in that water **(70)**. We have described the other things in that volume in which we set down the shores and divisions of the world.* But in order that knowledge of this sweat and labor of mine be plain to you, we will begin the narration of the work a bit more deeply **(77)**. You store in your innermost heart the things presented, for they are supported by knowledge sought and drawn from ancient sources.

The orb of the spreading earth lies extensively, and a wave in turn surrounds the earth **(80)**.+ But in the area from the Ocean where the deep salt water inserts itself so that here the swell of our sea extends far, there is the Atlantic gulf Here is the city Gadir, formerly called Tartessus **(85)**. Here are the columns of persistent Hercules, Abila and Calpe. The latter is on the left of the mentioned land; Abila is neighbor to Libya. They resound with the

---

*   Avienus refers to his *Descriptio Orbis Terrae,* which is based upon, but is not a literal translation of, Dionysius Periegetes. Avienus' poem is some 200 lines longer than Dionysius'.
+   With line 80 begins Avienus' first major division: the Northern and Western Seas (Ocean) to Spain. The treatment extends to line 171.

sept[r]ent(r)ione, sed loco certae tenent.
90 et prominentis hic iugi surgit caput,
Oestrymnin *istud dixit aevum antiquius,*
molesque celsa saxei fastigii
tota in tepentem maxime vergit notum.
sub huius autem prominentis vertice
95 sinus dehiscit incolis Oestrymnicus,
in quo insulae sese exerunt Oestrymniḍes,
laxe iacentes et metallo divites
stanni atque plumbi, multa vis hic gentis est,
superbus animus, efficax solertia,
100 negotiandi cura iugis omnibus,
netisque cumbis turbidum late fretum
eṭ beluosi gurgitem Oceani secant.
non hi carinas quippe, pinu texere
eṭ acere ṇoṛuṇt, non abiete, ut usus est,
105 curvant faselo(s), sed rei ad miraculum
navigia iunctis semper aptant pellibus
corioque vastum saepe, percurrunt salum.
ast hinc duobus in sacram, *sic* insulam
dixere prisci, solibus cursus rati est.
110 haec inter undas multa[m] caespitem iacet,
eamque late gens Hiernorum colit.
propinqua rursus insula Albionum patet.
Tartes(s)iisque in terminos Oestrumnidum
negotiandi mos erat. Carthaginis
115 etiam coloni[s] et vulgus inter Herculis
agitans columnas haec ad[h]ibant aequora,
quae Himilco Poenus mensibus vix quattuor,
ut ipse semet re[m] probasse re(t)tulit
enavigantem, posse transmitti adserit.

---

89 Septrentione 95 oestrymninus, *cf. v. 130* 101 netisque *Schulten:* nolusque 104 et acere *Klotz:* facere: acereve *Nonius* norunt *Nonius:* morem 105 faselos O: fasello 110 multa *Heinsius (cf. 152):* multam; multum caespitem iacit *Schulten cf.* Orb. *terr.* 496 hinc Campanus ager glaebam iacit 113 Tartesiis O: -sus 115 *del. Opitz* 117 paenus

harsh north wind, but remain firm in their places. Here rises the head of a projecting ridge, which a more ancient age' called Oestrymnis, and the lofty mass or rocky height completely faces the warm south wind **(93)**.

Under the head of this promontory, the Oestrymnic bay lies open for the natives. In it the islands called Oestrymnides stretch themselves out. They lie widely apart and are rich in tin and lead. There is much hardiness in the people here, a proud spirit, an efficient industriousness. They are all constantly concerned with commerce (100). They ply the widely troubled sea and swell of monster-filled Ocean with skiffs of skin. For these men do not know how to fashion keels with pine or maple. They do not hollow out yachts, as the custom is, from fir trees **(105)**. Rather they always marvellously fit out boats with joined skins and often run through the vast salt water on leather.

But from here, there is a two-day journey for a ship to the Holy Island-thus the ancients called it.* This island, large in extent of land, lies between the waves **(110)**. The race of Hierni inhabits it far and wide. Again, the island of the Albiones lies near, and the Tartessians were accustomed to carry on business to the ends of the Oestrymnides. Colonists of Carthage, too, and the common folk living around the Pillars of Hercules came to these seas **(116)**. Himilco of Carthage reported that he himself had investigated the matter on a voyage, and he asserts that it can scarcely be crossed

---

*   It is commonly, although not universally, held that Avienus is writing about Ireland and England in lines 108-12. It is curious that England is included as a sort of appendix to Ireland. This may reflect very ancient ties between Spain and Ireland or the ancients' misconception that Ireland lay to the west of Spain.

120	sic nulla late flabra propellunt ratem,
	sic segnis humor aequoris pigri stupet.
	adicit et illud: plurimum inter gurgites
	extare fucum et saepe virgulti vice
	retinere pup(p)im. dicit hic nihilominus
125	non in profundum terga demitti maris
	parvoque aquarum vix supertexi solum.
	obire semper huc et hu[n]c ponti feras,
	navigia lenta et languide repentia
	internatare beluas. siquis dehinc
130	ab insulis Oestrymnicis lembum audeat
	urgere in undas, axe qua Lycaonis
	rigescit aethra, caespitem Ligur[g]um subit
	cassum incolarum. namque Celtarum manu
	crebrisque dudum proeliis vacua arva sunt
135	Liguresque pulsi, ut saepe fors aliquos agit,
	venere in ista, quae per horrentis tenent
	plerumque dumos. creber his scrupus locis
	rigidaeque rupes atque montium minae
	caelo inseruntur. et fugax gens haec quidem
140	diu inter arta cautium duxit diem
	secreta ab undis. nam sali metuens erat
	priscum ob peric[u]lum, post quies et otium
	securitate roborante audaciam
	persuasit altis devehi cubilibus
145	atque in marinos iam locos descendere.
	post illa rursum quae supra fa[c]it sumus
	magnus patescit aequoris (fusi) sinus
	Ophius(s)am ad usque. rursum ab huius li[t]tore
	internum ad aequor, *qua mare insinuare se*
150	*dixi ante terris*, quodque Sardum nuncupant,
	septem dierum tenditur pediti via[e].
	Ophiussa porro tanta panditur latus
	quantam iacere Pelopis audis insulam

---

121 regnis   122 Adiicient illud   125 demitti *Hudson*: dimiti   134: vacua arva *Wernsdorf*: vacuata   146 supra *Opitz*: super   151 pediti *Burmann*: reditu del. *Hudson*

in four months. No breezes propel a craft, the sluggish liquid of the lazy sea is so at a standstill **(121)**. He also adds this: a lot of seaweed floats in the water and often after the manner of a thicket holds the prow back. He says that here nonetheless the depth of the water does not extend much and the bottom is barely covered over with a little water. They always meet here and there monsters of the deep, and beasts swim amid the slow and sluggishly crawling ships **(129)**.

If anyone should dare to drive his ship into the waves from here at the Oestrymnic Islands to where the air of Lycaon grows stiff, he enters the Ligurian land, empty of inhabitants. For because of a band of Celts and frequent battles, the fields have long been empty; and the routed Ligurians, as Fortune often drives some, came to those places which they possess generally in dense thickets **(137)**. There is much rock in these places, and rugged cliffs and threatening mountain peaks reach into the sky. And this fearful tribe, indeed, for a long time passed its days amid the narrow spaces of the crags, removed from the sea; for it feared the sea because of the ancient danger **(142)**. Afterwards, peace and quiet persuaded them to come down from their lofty homes and descend to the areas around the sea-security thus bolstered their daring **(145)**.

Then after the places that we spoke of above, the great bay of the wide sea opens all the way up to Ophiussa. Then from the shore of this latter to the inner sea, where I said before the sea folds itself into land, and which they call the Sea of the Sardi, there extends a journey of seven days for one on foot **(151)**. Ophiussa extends in breadth as much as you hear that the island of Pelops does in the land of the Greeks.*

---

*   The geographers are, of course, badly mistaken to think Spain (Ophiussa), even at the Pyrenees, is as wide as the Peloponnesus. Spain is much wider.

Graiorum in agro. haec dicta primo Oestrymnis (est)
155　locos et arva Oestrymnicis habitantibus,
post multa serpens effugavit incolas
vacuamque glaebam nominis fecit sui.
Procedit inde in gurites Veneris iugum
circumlatratque pontus insulas duas
160　tenue ob locorum inhospitas. Aryium
rursum tumescit prominens in asperum
septentrionem cursus aut(em) hinc classibus
usque in columnas efficacis Herculis
quinque est dierum. post pelagia est insula
165　herbarum abundans, ad(que) Saturno sacra.
sed vis in illa tanta naturalis est,
ut siquis hanc innavigando accesserit,
mox excitetur propter insulant more,
quatiatur ipsa et omne subsiliat salum
170　alte intremescens cetero ad stagni vicem
pelago silente. prominens surgit dehinc
Ophiussae in auras, abque Arui(i) iugo
in haec locorum bidui cursus patet.
at qui dehiscit inde prolixe sinus,
175　non totus uno facile navigabilis
vento recedit. namque medium ac(cess)eris
zephyro vehente, reliqua deposcunt notum.
et rusus inde si petat quisquam pede
Tartessiorum litus, exuperet viam
180　vix luce quarta. siquis ad nostrum mare
Malac(a)eque portum semitam tetenderit,
in quinque soles est iter. Ium Cempsicum
iugum intumescit. subiacet porro insula
Achale *vocata ab incolis. a(e)gre est*[i] *fides*

---

154 *add.* O 155 Locus 158 gurgites *Hudson*: -tis 159 insucas 161 promineas 162 Septentrionum *add. Opitz* 169 salum *Schulten*: solum 172 in auras *C. Müller*: moras 175 uno *Schrader*: uni vavigabilis 176 namque *Schrader*: nunquam *add. Schrader* 182 Cempsicum *Wernsdorf*: cepresicum 184 aegre est O: agresti

This place was first called Oestrymnis and the people inhabiting the area and the fields Oestrymnici. Afterwards numerous serpents put the inhabitants to flight and gave the evacuated land their name **(157)**.

Then the ridge of Venus proceeds out into the deep and the deep lashes about the two islands which are inhospitable because of the poverty of the locale. Next, the Aryian promontory swells toward the rough north. The passage, however, from here to the Pillars of powerful Hercules is five days for boats. After this there is an ocean island abounding in grass and sacred to Saturn **(165)**. But there is such natural force in the island that if someone approaches it by sailing, the sea around the island is stirred, the island itself is shaken, and all the salt water, roaring loudly, splashes up although the rest of the sea is as quiet as a swamp **(171)**.

From here the promontory of Ophiussa rears up into the air.* And the trip from the ridge of Arvium to this locale is two days. But the bay which spreads widely from there is not all easily navigable by one wind **(175)**. For you arrive at the middle of the bay with the west wind carrying you, the rest requires a south wind. And again if one should head for the Tartessian shore from there on foot, he would complete the journey scarcely on the fourth day **(180)**. If one prolongs his trip to our sea and the port of Malaca, the journey lasts for five days.

Then the Cempsican ridge rises up. But the island called by its inhabitants Achale lies beneath it. There is scarcely credi-

---

*   With line 172 begins Avienus' second major division: the Western Sea (Ocean) from Spain (Ophiussa) to Tartessus. The passage extends to line 261.

185	*narrationi[s] prae rei miraculo,*
	sed quam frequens auctoritas saṭ fulciat,
	aiunt in huius insulae confiniis
	numquam esse formam gurgiti reliquo parem.
	splendore(m) ubique quippe inesse fluctibus
190	vitri ad nitorem et per profundum marmoris
	coeaneam in undis esse certum imaginem est.
	confuṇdi at illic aequor immundọ luto
	memorant vetusti semper atque sordibus
	ut faeculentos gurgites haerescere.
195	Cempsi atque S[a]efes arduos collis habent
	Ophiussae in agro. propter hos pernix Ligus
	Draganumque proles sub nivosọ maxime
	septentrione conlocaverant larem.
	Poetanion autem est insula ad Sefum[um]latus
200	patulusque portus. inde Cempsis adiacent
	populi Cynetum. (tum) Cyneticum iugum,
	qua sideralis lucis inclinatio est,
	alte tumescens ditis Europae extimum
	in beluosi vergit Oceani [si] salum.
205	Ana aṃnis illic per Cynetas effluit
	sulcatque glaebam. panditur rursus sinus
	cavusque caespes in meridiem patet.
	memorato ab amṇi gemina sese flumina
	scindunt repente perque praedicti sinus
210	crassum liquorem—quippe pinguesci(t) luto
	omne hic profundum—lenta trudunt agmina.
	hic insularum semet alte subrigit
	vertex duarum. nominis minor indiga est,
	aliam vocavit mos tenax Agonida.

---

185 *del.* O 186 sal 190 profundam 191 coeaneam: cyaneam O 192 confundi at *Barth*: confodiat immundo O: -da 196 Ligus *Schrader*: lucis 197 nivoso O: -sa 198 conlocaverant: -runt *Klotz* 199 *del. C. Müller* latus *idem*: latet 201 *add. Opitz* tyneticum 203 cum escens 204 Im 205 animis 205-211 *ab Avieno loco moti, post 240 positi fuisse videntur* 208 ab amni *Unger*: aliamin 214 mox

bility for a story, due to its remarkable nature, but it rests on sufficiently frequent authority **(186)**. They say that on the confines of that island the appearance of the water is never like the rest of the swell. For everywhere else there is a gleam in the waves after the glint of glass and it is certain that there is a bluish image through to the bottom of the sea **(191)**. But there, the ancients recount that the sea is always churned up with dirty mud and the muddy waters are thick with filth **(194)**.

The Cempsi and the Sefes occupy the steep hills in the land of Ophiussa. Next to these, the quick Ligurian* and the offspring of the Draganes have situated their homes beneath the very snowy north wind. Poetanion, however, is an island on the flank of the Sefes and there is an open harbor **(200)**. From there the peoples of the Cynetes lie next the Cempsi. Then there is the Cynetican ridge. Rising high where the starlight sets, this extremity of rich Europe extends out into beast-filled Ocean's salt water **(204)**.

The Ana river flows out there through the Cynetes and furrows the land. Again the bay spreads out and hollow land extends to the south. From the aforementioned river, two branches suddenly divide and through the sluggish water of the abovementioned bay—for all this sea is thick with mud—follow their slow courses **(211)**. Here the tops of two islands raise themselves on high. The smaller one lacks a name, the other tenacious custom has called Agonis. Then there stands ruggedly on the cliffs a crag, and it too

---

*   "Ligurian" is a translation based on Schrader's emendation *Ligus*, which Schulten accepted, but which Berthelot has rejected, Berthelot suggests *Lusis* and sees in that people the ancestors of the Lusitanians.

215	inhorret inde rupibus cautes sacra
	Saturni et ipsa. fervet inlisum mare
	li[t]tusque late saxeum distenditur.
	hirtae hic capellae et multus incolis caper
	dumosa semper intererrant caespitum,
220	*castrorum in us[us]um et nauticis velamina*
	productiores [t]et graves setas alunt.
	hinc dictum ad amne(m) solis unius via est,
	genti et Cynetum hic terminus. Tartes(si)us
	ager his adh(a)eret adluitque caespitem
225	Tartes(s)us amnis. idde tenditur iugum
	Zephyro sacratum. denique arcis sum(m)itas
	Zephyris vocata. celsa sed [ad] fastigia
	iugo eriguntur vertici(s). multus tumor
	conscendit auras et supersidens quasi
230	caligo semper nubilum condit caput.
	regio omnis inde maxime herboso solo est,
	nebulosa iuge his incolis convexa sunt,
	coactus aer atque crassior dies
	noctisque more ros frequens. nulla, ut solet,
235	flabra inferuntur, nullus aethram discutit
	superne venti spiritus, pigra incu[m]bat
	caligo terras et solum late madet.
	Zephyridos arcem siquis excedat rate
	et inferatur gurgiti nostri maris,
240	flabris vehetur, protinus favoni(i).
	Iugum inde rursus et sacrum infernae deae
	divesque fanum, penetrat abstrusi cavi
	adytumque caecum. multa propter est palus
	E[t]rebea dicta. quin at Herbi civitas
245	*stetisse fertur his locis prisca die,*
	quae pr(o)eliorum absumpta (tem)pestatibus

---

217 late *Opitz*: latus 221 productio restet 228 vertices *Hudson*. -ci tumor *idem*: timor 229 supersidens *Wernsdorf*: super syderis 234 solea 244 Erebea *Schulten*: Etrephaea

is sacred to Saturn **(216)**. The sea beaten against it seethes and the rocky shore stretches out far and wide. Here shaggy she-goats and many a he-goat wander about for the inhabitants through the thickets of the land. They grow rather long and heavy bristles for the use of the camp and for sailors' cloaks **(221)**. From here to the river we mentioned it is a journey of one day. This is the boundary of the tribe of the Cynetes.

The Tartessian territory touches these and the' Tartessus river washes the land **(225)**. From here extends the ridge sacred to Zephyrus. Then there is the height of the citadel called Zephyris. The lofty heights of the peak rear up from the ridge. A great elevation rises up in the air, and as if brooding, a fog always hides the peak in clouds **(230)**. All the region from here is very grassy. Clouds are constantly drawn over these dwellers. The air is dense and the day rather humid, and there is frequent dew after the manner of night. No breezes are usually carried in, no breath of wind from above dispels the air **(235)**. A heavy fog lies upon the land and the earth is widely damp. If one were to leave from the citadel of Zephyris on a boat and be carried into the swell of our sea, he will be carried forward by the blasts of the west wind **(240)**.

From here then is the Sacred ridge of the infernal goddess* and the rich temple, the sanctuary of the remote cave, and the murky asylum. Nearby there is an extensive swamp called Erebea. Then too there is the city of Herbi. It is said to have stood in these places in days of oici **(245)**. Wasted by the blasts of war, it has left only its name and fame to the land. But the river Hiberus flows from here and enriches the land with its wave,

---

*   The cult of the infernal goddess and the underground sanctuary probably were native institutions.   The Phocaeans transferred the trappings of Tartarus to this western locale.

famam atque nomen sala, liquit caespiti.
at Hiberus inde manat amnis et locos
fecundat unda. *plurimi ex ipso ferunt*
250 *dictos Hiberos, non ab illo flumine*
quod inquietos [vo] Vasconas praelabitur.
nam quicquid amnem gentis huius adiacet
occiduum ad axem, Hiberiam cognominant.
pars portr eoa continet Tartes(s)ios
255 et Cilbicenos. Cartare post insula est
eamque pridem, influx(a) e(t est) satis [est] fides,
tenuere Cempsi. proximorum postea
pulsi duello, varia quaesitum loca
se protulere. Cassius inde mons tumet.
260 *et Graia ab ipso lingua cassiterum prius*
stannum vocavit. inde fani est prominens
et quae vetustum, Graeci(a)e nomen tenet,
Gerontis arx est eminus. *namque ex ea*
Geryona quondam, nuncupatum accepimus.
265 hic ora late sunt sinus Tartes(s)ii.
dictoque ab amni in haec locorum puppibus
via est diei. *Gadir hic est oppidum,*
nam Punicorum lingua cons(a)eptum locum,
Gadir vocabat. ipsa Tartessus *prius*
270 *cognomina(ta) est. multa et opulens civitas*
aevo vetusto, nunc egena, nunc brevis,
nunc destituta, nunc ruinarum ag(g)er est.
nos hic locorum, praeter Herculanea(m)
solemnitatem vidimus miri nihil.
275 *at vis in illis tanta vel tantum decus*
aetate prisca sub fide rerum fuit,
rex ut superbus omniumque. praepotens,
quos gens habebat forte tum Maurusia,

---

248 at *Opitz*: an 249 et 250 hybetos 251 uo uascomas 256 influxa et est satis *Wernsdorf*: influxe satis est 258 que est tum 263 ars 266 amni *Schulten*: uni: Ana *Müllenhoff* 273 hic *Klotz*: hoc 275 tamen

Very many say that the Hiberi* are named from this river, not from the one that glides by the restless Vascones **(251)**. For whatever people lies to the west of this river they call Hiberian. Its eastern part, however, contains the Tartessians and Cilbiceni. After it is the island Cartare, and there are sufficient grounds for believing that the Cempsi had held it. Afterwards, routed in war with their neighbors, they went forth to seek different places. Next the mountain Cassius rises up **(259)**. Because of this mountain, the Greek tongue formerly called tin "cassiterum."

Next there is a promontory of a temple and at a distance, a place which has an ancient Greek name, the citadel of Geron. + For we have received the report that once upon a time Geryon was named from it **(264)**. Here over a long distance is the shore of the Tartessian bay. From the river named above to these locales it is a journey of one day for boats. Here is the town Gadir, for it means in the language of the Carthaginians "fenced-in place." It was formerly called Tartessus **(270)**. In ancient times, it was a large and wealthy state, now it is poor, now it is small, now it is abandoned, now a heap of ruins. Here we saw nothing remarkable beyond the yearly rites of Hercules **(274)**. But there was such strength in them or such honor in days of yore, so it is believed, that a proud and most powerful king of all those who then happened to control the Mauretanian race, and a king most acceptable

---

*   The spellings "Hiberi" and "Hiberian" are retained because those are Avienus' forms of the words.
+   With line 261 begins the third major division of Avienus' work: the description of Tartessus and its environs. It extends to line 317. The passage has stirred more controversy than any other section of the poem.

Octaviano principi acceptissimus
280 *et lit(t)erarum semper in studio Iuba*
interfluoque separatus aequore,
inlustriorem semet urbis istius
duumviratu crederet. sed insulam
Tartessus amnis ex Ligustino lacu
285 per aperta fusus undique adlapsu ligat.
neque iste tractu simplici provolvitur
unusve sulcat subiacentem caespitem,
tria ora quippe parte eoi luminis
infert in agros, ore bis gemino quoque
290 meridiana civitatis adluit.
at mons paludem incu(m)bit Argentarius
sic a vetustis dictus ex specie sui.
stagno isle namque latera plurimo nitet
magisque in auras eminus lucem evomit,
295 *cum sol ab igni celsa perculerit iuga.*
idem amnis aut(em) fluctibus stagni gravis
ramenta volv(i)t invehitque moenibus
dives metallum. qua dehinc ab aequore
salsi fluenti vasta per medium soli
300 regio re(ce)dit, gens Etmaneum accolit.
atque inde rursus usque Cempsorum sata
Ileates agro se feraci porrigunt.
maritima vero Ci(l)biceni possident.
Gerontis arcem et prominens fani, ut supra
305 *sumus elocuti, distinet medium salum*
interque celsa cautium cedit sinus.
iugum ad secundum flumen amplum amplum evolvit(ur).
Tartes(s)iorum mons dehinc attollitur
silvis opacus. hinc Erythia est insula
310 diffusa gl(a)ebam et iuris olim Punici.
habuere primo quippe eam Cart(ha)ginis

---

283 Duum iuratu 285 adlapsu *Hudson*: ablapsu 296 *add. Hudson*
300 *add. Hudson* 303 *add. Hudson* 307 *add. Hudson* 310 uiris.

to Octavian the *princeps,* Juba, who was always occupied with the pursuit of letters,* though separated by the intervening sea, thought he made himself more illustrious by the duumvirate of that city **(283)**.

But the Tartessus river, spread through open spaces from the Ligustine lake, binds an island on all sides with its lapping. Nor does the river flow through with a simple course or singly cleave the underlying earth. Rather, on the eastern side, it brings three mouths into the fields, and it washes the south part of the city with four mouths **(290)**. But the mountain Argentarius looms over the swamp. Thus it was called by the ancients from its appearance. For its sides gleam due to great deposits of tin, and it reflects the light at a distance into the air even more when the fiery sun hits its lofty ridges **(295)**. The same river, however, rolls down with its waves pieces of heavy tin and brings rich metal to the city walls.

Next where a vast region of land recedes from the sea of flowing salt water, the Etmaneum race dwells **(300)**. And from there in turn all the way to the fields of the Cempsi, the Ileates extend themselves on a fertile land. But the Cibiceni hold the seashore lands. As we said above, salt water in the middle separates the citadel of Geron and the promontory of the temple, and a bay recedes between the heights of the crags **(306)**. At the second ridge, an ample river flows out. Then the mountain of the Tartessians rises up, dark with forests. Next is the island of Erythia, spread in its land and once under Punic sway **(310)**. For at first, colonists of old Carthage possessed it, but Erythia is cut off from the mainland by the intervening sea at a distance of five

---

* Juba II (c. 50 B.C.-c. 23 A.D.), king of Mauretania, wrote many books in Greek. They are now lost save for fragments. Their scope included the history of Rome, comparison of Greek and Roman antiquities, and works on Libya, Arabia, and Assyria.

prisc(a)e coloni interfluoque scinditur
a[t] continente[m] quinque per stadia mari
Erythia. ab arce qua diei occasus est,
315 Veneri marinae consecrata est insula
templumque in illa Veneris et penetral cavum
oraculumque. *monte ab illo, quent tibi
horrere. silvis dixeram, cum veneris,*
litus recline et molle harenarum iacet,
320 in quas Besilus atque Cilbus flumina
urgent fluentum. post in occiduum diem
Sacrum superbas erigit cautes iugum.
*locum, hunc vocavit Herma quondam Graecia.
est Herma porr[h]o caespitum munitio,*
325 *interfluumque altrinsecus munit lacum.
aliique rursus Herculis dicunt[ur ani] viam.
stravisse quippe maria fertur Hercules,
iter ut pateret facile captivo gregi.
porr[h]o illud Herma iure sub Libyci soli*
330 *fuisse pridem plurimi auctores ferunt.
nec respuendus testis est Dionysius,
Liby(a)e esse finem qui docet Tartessium.
Europ(a)e in agro, quod vocari ab incolis
Sacrum indicavi, prominens subducitur.*
335 locos utrosque interfluit tenue fretum.
quod Herma porr[h]o aut Herculis dictum est via,
Amphipolis urbis incola Euctemon ait,
non plus h(ab)ere longitudinis modo
quam porriguntur centum et octo milia
340 et distineri (terras) milibus tribus.
hic Herculanae stant columnae, *quas modum
utriusque haberi continentis legimus.*
sunt paria porr[h]o saxa prominentia

---

313 a continente *Müllenhoff*: at continentem mari *Klotz*: modo 316 poene sal 318 cum *v. Gutschmid*: in 319 redine 321 urgent *Opitz*: vergent 325 lacum *Wernsdorf*: locus 329 libyque 335 locos O: locus 337 Euctemon O: hoc demon 340 *add. Klotz* 343 *paria Burmann*: parva

stades. To the west of the citadel, there is an island consecrated to Venus of the Sea and on it there is a temple of Venus, an inner sanctuary, and an oracle (317).

When you come from that mountain which I said was thick with forests, you find a receding and sandy shore in which the rivers Besilus and Cilbus press the sea.* After that on the west, the Sacred ridge rears up proud crags. Once upon a time Greece called this place Herma. Herma, of course, is an earthern fortification, and it fortifies from both sides a lake that flows between its arms (325). Others again state it is the route of Hercules, for Hercules is said to have split the seas in order to open an easy path for his captured flock. Further, very many authors report that Herma was once under the yoke of the Libyan land (330). Nor is Dionysius to be spurned as a witness, who points out that Tartessus is the boundary of Libya. On the land of Europe, a promontory follows, which I indicated was called by the inhabitants Sacred. A narrow sea flows between both places (335). Euctemon, an inhabitant of Amphipolis,+ says the place this called Herma or the way of Hercules extends no more than 108 miles and that it is three miles wide.

Here stand the Pillars of Hercules, which we read are the boundaries of both continents. For there are similar rock promontories, Abila and Calpe. Calpe is on the Spainish soil, Abila

---

*　　With the latter part of line 317 begins the fourth major division of Avienus' description: the Spanish coast from Tartessus to Cape Nao. The division extends to line 471.

+　　Elsewhere at lines 47-48 and 350, Euctemon is said to be an Athenian. Cf. the commentary *ad hunc locum.*

	Abil[l]a atque Calpe. *Calpe (in) Hispano solo,*
345	*Maurusiorum est Abil[l]a. namque Abil[l]lam vocant*
	gens Punicorum, mons quod altus barbaro est,
	id est Latino, dic[t]i ut au(c)tor Plautus est.
	Calpeque rursum in Graecia species cavi
	teretisque visu nuncupatur urcei.
350	Atheniensis dicit Euctemon item
	non esse saxa aut vertices adsurgere
	parte ex utraque. caespitem Libyci soli
	Europae et oram memorat insulas duas
	i(n)ter(i)acere; nuncupari has Herculis
355	ait columnas; [e]stadia tri[t]ginta refert
	has distinere; horrere silvis undique
	inhospita[ta]sque semper esse nauticis.
	inesse quippe dicit ollis Herculis
	et templa et [h]aras. invehi advenas rate[s],
360	deo litare, abire festino pede,
	nefas putatum demorari in insulis.
	circum atque iuxta plurimo (tractu iacens)
	manere tradit tenue prolixe mare.
	navigia [h]onusta adire non valent locos
365	breve ob fluentum et pingue lit[t]ori(s) lutum.
	sed si voluntas forte quem subegerit
	adire fanum, prop[t]er(at) ad Lunae insulam
	agere carinam, eximere classi pondera,
	levique cymba sic superferri salo.
370	sed ad columnas quicquid interfunditur
	und(a)e aestuantis, stadia septem vix ait
	Damastus esse. Caryandaeus Scylax
	medium fluentum inter columnas adserit
	tantum patere quantus aestus Bosp[h]oro est.
375	ultra has columnas propter Europae latus
	vicos et urbis incolae Carthaginis
	tenuere quondam. mos at ollis hic erat,
	ut planior(e) texerent fundo rates,

---

345 Maurisiorum Abilam *Salmasius*: ab illa 348 cavi *Nonius*: cava 349 teretisque *Nonius*: -esque -urcei *Salmasius*: et iugi 354 interiacere *Barth*: Iter acervi 359 del. *Heinsius* 362 add. *Hudson* 365 litoris O: litteri 369 sic *Wernsdorf*: vix 371 studia 372 Damascus: cariae dictus 373 columnas 375 latet

on the Mauretanians' **(345)**. For the Carthaginian race calls Abila that which in a barbarous—Plautus is the authority for this— tongue, that is Latin, is "high mountain." Calpe, in turn, in Greece is a kind of hollow and round-looking pitcher **(349)**. Euctemon of Athens further says that they are not rocks nor do peaks rise up on both sides. He says that two islands lie between the land of Libyan soil and the shore of Europe; he says these are called the Pillars of Hercules. He reports that these stand 30 stades apart and that they are thick with trees and are always inhospitable to sailors **(357)**. He says that there are indeed temples and altars of Hercules on them. Visiting ships sail in, offer sacrifice to the god, and quickly speed away **(360)**. It is thought a sacrilege to tarry on the islands. He reports that a very shallow sea with great extent lies around and next to them. Transports cannot approach these places because of the shallowness of the sea and the thick mud of the shore **(365)**. But if one's will prompts him to approach the shrine, he hastens to direct his ship to the island of the Moon, to take all the weight off the boat, and thus be carried over the sea in a light ship.

But as to the amount of swirling sea between the Pillars, Damastus* says there are scarcely seven stades. Scylax of Caryanda asserts that the water between the Pillars extends as much as the sea does in the Bosporus. Beyond these Pillars on the European side, inhabitants of Carthage once possessed villages and cities **(377)**. But their custom was to weave boats of flatter bottom so that the wider boat might glide better over the shallower

---

*   Damastes is the more correct form of the name.

           quo cymba tergum fusior brevius maris
380   praelaberetur. porro in occiduam plaga(m)
           ab his columnis gurgitem esse interminum,
           late patere pelagus, extendi salum
           Himilco tradit. nullus haec adiit freta,
           nullus carinas aequor illud intulit,
385   desint quod alto flabra propellentia
           nullusque puppim spiritus caeli iuvet
           dehinc quod aethram quod(am) amictu vestiat
           caligo, se(m)per nebula condat gurgitem
           et crassiore[m] nubilum perstet die.
390   *Oceanus iste est, orbis effusi procul*
           circumlatrator, iste. pontus maximus,
           hic gurges oras ambi[g]ens, hic intimi
           salis inrigator, hic parens nostri maris.
           plerosque quippe extrinsecus curvat sinus
395   *nostrumque in orbem vis profundi inlabitur.*
           sed nos loquemur maximo(s) tibi qu(a)ttuor.
           prima huius ergo in caespitem insinuatio est
           Hesperius aestus atque Atlanticum salum;
           Hyrcana rursus unda, Caspium mare;
400   *salum Indicorum, terga, fluctus Persici;*
           Arabsque gurges sub tepente iam noto.
           hunc usus olim dixit Occanum vetus.
           Hyrcana rursus unda, Caspium mare;
           longo explicatur gurges huius ambitu
405   *produciturque latere prolixe vago.*
           Plerumque porro tenue tenditur salum,
           ut vix harenas subiacenti(s) occulat.
           exuperat autem gurgitem fuens frequens
           atque impeditur aestus hic uligine.
410   vis beluar[i]um pelagus omne, internatat
           multusque terror ex feris habitat freta.
           haec olim Himilco Poenus Oceano super

---

379 maris *Wernsdorf*: mare 381 colunnis 386 vivet 388 *add. Heinsius* 389 *del. Barth.* 391 circumlatrator *Hudson*: -tur 394 curvat *Schrader*: turbat 400 salum *Heinsius*: solo fluctus *Hudson*: -um 408 fucus *Hudson*: fusus 410 belluarum *Barth*: vel varium 412 hemelco

sea. **(380)*** But to the west of these Pillars, Himilco reports that the swell is boundless, the sea extends widely, the salt water stretches forth. No one has approached these waters, no one has brought his keel into that sea because there are no propelling breezes at sea, and no breath of heaven's air aids the ship. Hence because a mist cloaks the air with a kind of garment, a cloud always holds the swell and persists throughout a rather humid day **(389)**.

That is the Ocean which pounds the far-flung world. That is the great deep, this the swell that encircles the shores. This is the supplier of the inner salt water, this the parent of our sea. For from outside it carves several bays and the power of the deep glides into our world **(395)**. But we will mention to you the four greatest gulfs. The first of these, therefore, is the insertion into land by the Hesperian tide and Atlantic salt water; [2] then the Hyrcanian wave, the Caspian sea; [3] the sea of the Indians and the surface of the Persian wave; [4) the Arabian swell beneath the now warm south wind. Old usage said once that this last was the Ocean; then again the Hyrcanian wave, the Caspian sea. The Ocean's swell unfolds with long extend and is widely diffused with its wandering shore **(405)**. But very often the salt water extends so shallowly that it scarcely covers the underlying sands. Thick seaweed often tops the sea and the tide is hindered by marshy wrack. Many a beast swims through all the sea and great fear of monsters stalks the deep **(411)**. Himilco the Carthaginian reported that he had once seen and tested these things on the Ocean. These things published long ago in the secret annals of the Carthaginians*

---

*   The text is obscure here, but the meaning seems to be that the Carthaginian settlers around the Pillars of Hercules adjusted their shipbuilding methods to the difficult conditions of the sea in those parts.

spectasse semet et probasse re(t)tulit.
haec nos ab imis Punicorum annalibus
415 *prolata longo tempore edidimus tibi.*
nunc iam, recursus ad priora sit stilo.
igitur columnae, ut dixeram, Libystidis
Europae in agro adversa surgit altera.
hic Chrysus amnis intrat altum gurgitem,
420 ultra citraque quattuor gentes colunt.
nam sunt feroces hoc Libyphoenices loco,
sunt Massieni, regna C̣ịlbic̣enẹ sunt
feracis agri et divites Tartes(s)ii,
qui porriguṇtur in Calacticum sinum.
425 hos propter autem mox iugum Barbetium est
Malachaeque flumen urbe cum cognomina
Men[e]ace *prior(e quae) vocata est saeculo.*
Tartes(s)iorum ịụris illic insula
antistaṭ urbem, Noctilucae ab incolis
430 sacrata pridem. in insula stagnum quoque
tụtusque porṭus. oppidum Menace super.
qua sese ab undis regio dicta subtrahit,
Silurus alto mons tumet cacumine.
adsurgit inde vasta cautes et mare
435 intrat profundum. pinus *hanc quondam frequens*
ex se vocari sub sono Graio dedit.
fanumque ad usque Veneris ac Veneris iugum
lit[t]us recumbit. porro in isto lit[t]ore
stetere crebrae civitates antea
440 Phoenixque multus habuit hos pridem locos.
inhospitales nunc harenas porrigit
desertạ tellus, orba cultorm sola
squalent iacentque. Veneris ab di(c)to iugo

---

421 Libyphoenices loco *Schrader*: loci liby phoenices   422 Cilbicena *Schulten*: selbyssina   423 divites *Schrader*: -tis   424 porrigitur   427 Maeneace   428 viris   429 antistat nectilucae   431 tutusque *Heinsius*: totusque portus *Wernsdorf*: porrus   Menace *Bochart*: minace   435 profundam   442 deserat   443 *add. Hudson*

we have put forth to you. Now let our pen return to the earlier topics **(416)**.

Opposite the Libyan column, as I said, there rises in the land of Europe another. Here the Chrysus river enters the deep swell; four tribes dwell on this side and that **(420)**. For the fierce Libyphoenicians are in this place. + There are the Massieni; there is the kingdom Cilbicene, which has fertile land. And the rich Tartessians are there. These last extend to the Calactican bay **(424)**.

Next to these there is soon the Barbetian ridge and the river Malacha with a city of that same name. Formerly it was called Menace. There an island under sway of Tartessus lies opposite that city. It was in time past made sacred to Noctiluca by its inhabitants. On the island there is a lagoon and a safe port. The town Menace is above it **(431)**. Where the named region draws itself back from the waves, the mountain Silurus swells with lofty top. Then a vast crag rises up and enters the deep sea **(435)**. The pine that once was frequent here gave the crag its name in the Greek tongue. ⸸ The shore recedes all the way to the temple of Venus and the ridge of Venus. But on this shore frequent cities formerly stood, and many Phoenicians held these lands of old **(440)**. The deserted earth now extends inhospitable sands. The lands bereft of crops lie neglected. From the aforementioned ridge of Venus, Herma of the Libyan land, as I said before, is seen at

---

* Almost all scholars consider it unlikely that Avienus had direct access to Himilco's account of the northwestern sea.
+ "Libyphoenicians" is a vague term that Pliny uses of the people around the Syrtes in Africa (V. 24). Perhaps it means Phoenician colonists from Africa.
⸸ The Greek word alluded to is Pityussa.

spectator Herma caespitis Libyci procul,
445 *quod ante dixi.* lit[t]us hic rursum patet
vacuum, incolarum nunc et abieci soli.
porro ante et urbes hic stetere plurimae
populique multi concelebra(ru)nt locos.
Namnatius inde portus op(pidum pro)pe
450 se Massienum curvat alto ab aequore
sinuque in imo surgit altis moenibus
urbs Massiena. post iugum Tr[a]ete eminet
brevisque iuxta Strongyle stat insula.
dehinc in huius insulae confinis
455 immensa tergum latera diffundit palus.
Theodorus illic—*nec stupori sit ibi*
quod in feroci barbaroque. s[t]at loco
cognomen huius Graeciae accipis sono—
prorepit amnis. ista Phoenices prius
460 loca incolebant. rursus hinc se lit[t]oris
fundunt harenae et lit[t]us hoc tres insulae
cinxere late. hic terminus quondam stetit
Tartes(s)iorum, hic Herna civitas fuit.
Gymnetes istos gens locos insederant
469 *(Si)cani ad usque pr(a)efluentis alveum,*
465 nunc destitutus et diu incolis carens
sibi sonorus Alebus amnis effluit.
post haec per undas insula est Gymnesia,
populo incolarum quae vetus nomen dedit,
470 Pityuss(a)e et inde proferunt sese insulae
Baliari[car]um (ac) late insularum dorsa sunt.
et conta Hiberi in usque Pyren(a)e iugum
ius protulere propter interius mare
late locati. prima eorum civitas
475 Ilerda surgit. lit[t]us extendit dehinc
steriles harenas. Hemeroscopium quoque

---

449 *add. Wernsdorf* 452 *del. Müllenhoff* 457 *del. Hudson* 499 *ante* 466 *transposuit Schulten* 469 Sicani ad usque *idem:* ad usque cani 470 Pytuisse 471 *del. et add. Hudson* 473 protollere 474 locuti

a distance. Here in turn, the shore stands empty of inhabitants and now is a worthless spot. But formerly both many cities stood here, and many people thronged the places **(448)**.

Then the Namnatian port near the town of the Massieni curves in from the deep sea, and the Massienan city rises with high walls on the inmost bay. After this the ridge Trete stands forth and next to it stands the tiny island Strongyle. Then bordering on this island is an enormous lagoon that spreads its sides **(455)**. There the Theodorus—nor should you be amazed that there in a fierce and barbarous place stands a name of the Greek tongue—a river, issues forth. The Phoenicians formerly dwelled in those places **(460)**. Then from here the sands of the shore extend and three islands gird this shore over a long distance. This once stood as the boundary of the Tartessians. Here was the city Herna. The race of the Gymnetes had occupied those lands all the way to the bed of the Sicanus that flows by. Now it is deserted and for a long time lacks inhabitants **(465)**. The Alebus river, roaring to itself, flows out. After these places through the waves is the island Gymnesia, which gave an ancient name to the inhabiting people. Then the Pityussae islands project themselves, and far out to sea are the backs of the Baliares islands **(471)**.

And beyond here the Hiberi extend their power all the way to the ridge of Pyrene.* They are spread far and wide along the inner sea. The first city of theirs that rises up is Ilerda. The shore then spreads out sterile sands. Also a city Hemeroscopium was formerly inhabited here. Now the area, devoid of dwellers,

---

*   With line 472, the fifth major division of Avienus begins. It covers the Spanish shore from Cape Nao all the way to the Rhone. It extends to line 621.

habita(ta) pridem hic civitas. *nunc iam solum*
vacuum incolarum languido stagno madet.
attolit inde se Sicana civitas,
480   propinquo ab amini sic vocata Hibericis.
neque longe ab huius fluminis divortio
praestringit amnis Tyrius oppidum Tyrin.
at qua recedit ab salo tellus procul,
dumosa late terga regio porrigit.
485   Berybraces illic, gens agrestis et ferox,
pecorum frequentis intererrabat greges.
hi[c] lacte semet atque pingui caseo
praedure alentes proferebant spiritum
vicem ad ferarum. post Crabrasiae iugum
490   procedit alte ac nuda lit[t]orum iacent
ad usque Onussae (C)herronesi terminos.
palus per illa Naccararum extenditur.
hoc nomen isti nam pal(udi m)os dedit
stagnique medio parva surgit insula
495   ferax olivi et hinc Minerv(a)e s(t)at sacra.
fuere propter civitates plurimae.
quippe hic Hylactes Hystra Sarna et nobiles
Tyrichae stetere. *nomen oppido vetus,*
gazae incolarum maxime memorabiles,
500   per orbis oras. namque praeter caespitis
fecunditatem, qua pecus, qua palmitem,
qua dona flavae Cereris educat solum,
peregrina *Hibero* sub(v)e(h)untur flumine.
iuxta superbum mons (S)acer caput exerit
505   Oleumque flumen proxuma agrorum secans
geminos iugorum vertices interfluit.
mons quippe Sellus *nomen hoc monti est vetus,*
ad usque celsa nubium subducitur

---

479 Sicana *Voss:* sitana 481 ad 483 solo 491 Onussae Schulten: cassae 495 *add. Opitz* 497 nobilis 499 gazae *Wernsdorf:* Gaiae 500 Pre 504 *add. Schulten* 505 flumem 507 mons *Schulten:* Mox

inhabited here. Now the area, devoid of dwellers, is marshy with sluggish swamp **(478)**.

Next rises up the city Sicana, called this by the Hiberians from a nearby river. Not far from the split of this river, the Tyrius river touches the town Tyris. But where the land recedes far from the salt water, the region extends its widely thicketed backwoods **(485)**. There the Berybraces, a rough and fierce race, wander among frequent herds of stock. These men, nourishing themselves very hardily with milk and rich cheese, maintain their lives after the manner of wild beasts.*

After this the ridge of Crabrasia extends up loftily and the shores lie bare all the way to the boundaries of Onussa Cherronesus **(491)**. + The swamp of the Naccarares extends through those places. Custom has given this name to that swamp, and a small island rises up in the midst of the swamp. It is rich in olives and hence is sacred to Minerva **(495)**. There were very many cities nearby. For here stood Hylactes, Hystra, Sarna, and the famous Tyrichae. Tyrichae was the ancient name of the town. For beyond the fertility of the land, by which the area produces cattle, the palm, and the gifts of golden Ceres, foreign goods are carried up the river Hiberus **(503)**.

Nearby, the Sacred mountain puts forth its proud head, and the Oleum river, cutting through the closed fields, flows between twin sets of ridges. For indeed, Mount Sellus–that is the ancient name for this second mountain–climbs up the heights of the clouds, and the city Lebedontia stood next to it in an earlier age. Now the

---

* The phrase *vicem adferarum* may also mean "instead of wild beasts." That is, the Berybraces substituted milk and cheese for meat in their diets.

+ Onussa Cherronesus is an emendation proposed by Schulten. Cf. the critical apparatus and commentary.

adstabat istum civitas Lebedontia
510　*priore (s)aeclo, nunc ager vacu[i]us lare.*
　　lustra et ferarum sustinet cubilia.
　　post haec harenae plurimo tractu iacent,
　　per quas Salauri(s) *oppidum quondam stetit,*
　　in quis et olim prisca Callipolis *fuit,*
515　Callipolis ill(a, quae per altam) m(o)enium
　　proceritatem et celsa[m] per fastigia
　　subibat auras, quae laris vasti ambitu
　　latere ex utroque piscium ferax
　　stagnum [im]premebat. *inde Tarraco oppidum*
520　*et Barcilonum amoena[s] sedes ditium.*
　　nam pandit illic tuta portus brachia,
　　uvetque semper dulcibus tellus aquis.
　　post Indigetes asperi se proferunt,
　　gens ista dura, gens ferox venatibus
525　lustrisque inh(a)erens. tum iugum Celebanticum
　　in usque salsam dorsa porrigit Thetim.
　　hic adstitisse civitatem Cypselam
　　iam fama tantum est. nulla nam vestigia
　　prioris urbis asperum servat solum.
530　dehiscit illic maximo portus sinu
　　cavumque late c(a)espitem inrepit salum.
　　post qu(a)e recumbit lit[t]us Indiceticum.
　　Pyren(a)e ad usque prominentis verticem.
　　post lit[t]us illud, quod iacere diximus
535　*tractu supino,* se Malodes exerit
　　mons inter undas (et) tument sco(puli duo)
　　geminusque ver(tex celsa nubium petit).
　　hos inter aut(em) portus effuse iacet
　　nullisque flabris aequor est obnoxium.
540　sic omne, late praelocatis rupibus,

---

510 aedo 512 tracta 513 *add. Hudson* 515 illa O: ill *add. Opitz* 519 premebat *Hudson*: imprimebat carraco 525 Celebanticum *Schulten*: celebandicum 536 *add. Schulten*: sco(puli) iam *Wernsdorf*: 537 *add. Wernsdorf* 538 *add. Hudson*

area is devoid of household gods and endures the wanderings and lairs of wild beasts **(511)**. After these, sands lie over a vast tract through which the town Salauris once stood. In these too once was old Callipolis. That famous Callipolis rose up into the sky because of her lofty walls and high pinnacles. Due to the vast extent of its habitation, Callipolis on both sides borders a sea that is rich in fish **(519)**.

Then there is the town Terraco and the pleasant seat of the rich Barcilones. For there the port opens out safe arms, and the land is always supplied with fresh water. After these, the rough Indigetes present themselves, that harsh race, that fierce people, engaging in the hunt and nomadic life **(525)**. Then the Celebantican ridge extends its back all the way to the salty sea. Now only the rumor remains that once the city Cypsela had stood there. For the rough land preserves no vestiges of the former city **(529)**.

There the port gapes open with a very large bay, and the sea creeps widely into the hollow land. After this the shore of the Indicetes reclines all the way to the top of the promontory Pyrene **(533)**. After that shore which we said lies with backward tract, Mount Malodes pushes itself out into the waves and two crags* swell up, and twin peaks seek the heights of the clouds. Between these peaks, however, a port lies spread and the sea is subject to no breezes. Thus since the cliffs extend far out, the tops of the

---

* As the critical apparatus shows, these lines abound in scholars' emendations of the faulty Pisanus text. The emendation *scopuli magni* of Lamboglia would mean "large crags," but has the serious shortcoming of ending the iambic line with two long syllables.

latus ambiere cautium cacumina,
interque saxa immobilis gurges latet,
quiescit aequor, pelagus inclusum stupet.
stagnum inde Toni montium in radicibus
545 Tononitaeque attolitur ru[m]pis iugum.
per quae sonorus volvit aequor spumeum
Anystus amni(s) et salum fluctu secat.
haec propter undas atque salsa sunt freta,
at quicquid agri cedit alto a gurgite,
550 C[a]eretes omne et Auṣoceretes prius
habuere duri, nunc pari sub nomine
gens est Hiberum. Ṣordus inde denique
populus agebat inter avios locos
ac pertinentes usque ad interius mare
555 qua pinifer[t]ae stant Pyrenae vertices
inter ferarum lustra duceba(nt diem)
et arva late et gurgitem ponti premu̱nt.
in Sordiceni caespitis confinio
quondam Pyren[a]e [latera] civitas ditis laris
560 *stetisse fertur*, hicque Mas(s)iliae incolae
negotiorum saepe versabant vices.
sed in Pyrenen *ab columnis Herculis
Atlanticoque gurgite et confinio
Zephyri(di)s orae* cursus est celeri rati
565 septem dierum. post Pyrenaeum iugum
iacent harenae lit[t]oris Cynetici,
easque late sulcat amnis Rhoscynus.
hoc Sordicenae, ut diximus, glaeb(a)e solum est.
stagnum hic palusqu[a]e quippe diffus[a]e patet,

---

544 Tonon *Hudson* 547 *add. Hudson* 550 Ausoceretes *Unger*: aucoceretes 552 Sordus *Hudson:* cor dus 555 *post* 556 *posuit Schrader* 556 *add. Schrader* 555 *del. Meincke* 557 premunt *Müllenhoff:* premit 559 *del. Pithou* ditis laris *Pithou*: diti flaris 562 colunnis 564 *add. Heinsius* 567 Rhoscynus *Unger*: roschinus

rocks embrace every side, and the swell lies immoble between the rocks, the sea grows quiet and the enclosed surface is calm **(543)**.

Next there is the lagoon Toni at the feet of the mountains and the ridge of the Tononitan cliff rises up. Through these the loud river Anystus churns the foamy sea and cuts the salt water with its flood. These waters because of the waves are also salty. But whatever land lies behind the deep swell, the harsh Ceretes and Ausoceretes formerly held **(550)**. Now a race with common name holds them—the Hiberi. Next the Sordan people live amid intractable places and extend all the way to the interior sea where the pine-bearing heads of Pyrene stand **(555)**. They spend their days among the lairs of beasts and exploit the fields and swell of the deep over a large area. It is said that once upon a time the city Pyrene,* a prosperous town, stood upon the boundary of the Sordicene land **(560)**. Here citizens of Massilia often carried on business. But the run to Pyrene from the Pillars of Hercules, the Atlantic swell and the boundary of Zephyris is, for a fast ship, seven days long **(565)**.

After the ridge of Pyrene, there lie the sands of the Cynetic shore, and the river Rhoscynus widely furrows them. This, as we said, is the land of the Sordi. Here there is a lagoon and swamp that spreads over a large area. The natives call it Sordices **(570)**. And beyond the noisy waters of the vast swell—for because of the large extent of its undefined edge, the lagoon often swells with driving winds—the Sordus river flows out from this very place.

---

*   The exact identification of Pyrene is disputed, cf. the commentary. At any rate it was a trading station for Massiliot merchants as the text of Avienus clearly indicates.

570	et incolae istam Sordicem *cognominant*.
	praeterque vasti gurgitis crepulas aquas
	—nam propter amplum marginis lax(a)e ambitum
	ventis tumescit saepe (per)cellentibus—
	stagno hoc ab ipso Sordus amnis effluit.
575	ru(rsusque ab huius) effluentis [h]ostiis
	. . . .
	. . . . (litus dehinc)
	sinuatur alto et propria per dispendia
	caespes cavatur, [e]repit unda largior
580	molesque multa gurgitis distenditur.
	tris namque in illo maximae stant insulae
	saxisque duris pelagus interfunditur.
	nec longe ab isto caespitis rupti sinus
	alter dehiscit insulasque qu(a)ttuor
585	—*at priscus usus dixit has omnis* Piplas—
	ambit profundo. gens Elesycum prius
	loca haec tenebat atque Naro civitas
	era(t) ferocis maximum regni caput.
	hic salsum in aequor amnis Attagus ruit
590	Heliceque rursus hic palus iuxta. dehinc
	Besaram *stetisse fama casca tradidit*.
	at nunc Heledus, nunc et Orobus flumina
	vacuos per agros et ruinarum aggeres
	amoenitatis indices priscae meant.
595	nec longe ab istis Thyrius alto evolvitur
	. . . +cinorus agmen . . . .
	. . . .
	. . . .
	numqua(m) excitent(ur) fluctuum volumina
600	sternatque semper gurgitem Alcyonae quies.
	vertex at huius cautis e regione se

---

575 *add*. Müllenhoff 577 *add*. Unger 579 repit *Schrader*: eripit 590 iuxta O: iusta 591 casca *Opitz*: cassa 596 cinorus: sonorus *Unger* 599 *add*. *Opitz* 601 ad

Then from the mouth of this river[1] ...* The shore then is curved by the deep and the land is hollowed by its own losses. The wave moves on more abundant and the great weight of the swell spreads out **(580)**. In it stand three very large islands and the sea is broken by hard rocks. Not far from there a second bay of broken earth opens up and encircles with water four islands, which, however, ancient usage called Piplae **(585)**. Formerly the tribe of Elesyces held these places and the city Naro was the great head of a fierce realm. Here the river Attagus rushes down into the salty sea. Then nearby is the swamp Helice **(590)**. Next, old custom has handed it down, stood Besara. But now the rivers Heledus and Orobus, signs of ancient beauty, pass through the empty fields and heaps of ruins. Not far from them the Thyrius rolls into the sea[2]. +
The waves are never disturbed and the calm of Alcyone always covers the sea. But the top of this crag extends out from that region to the promontory which I said was called Candidum **(603)**. Nearby is the island Blasco and the land is put forth into the sea

---

* Since the text of Avienus' *Ora Maritima* is completely dependent upon the *editio princeps* of Pisaunus, these short lacunae toward the end of the book cannot be filled. Most likely the manuscript from which the edition was made was damaged in these places or already contained the lacunae.

+ I have not translated the *cinorus agmen* which can be made out in the *editio princeps*. If Unger's emendation *sonorus* is accepted, the phrase might modify the Thyrius and mean "resounding in its course."

1. Two lines have been lost. cf *ed. princeps* p. 116.
2. Three lines have been lost. cf. *ed. princeps* p. 116.

illi eminenti porrigit, *quod* Candidum
dixi vocari. Blasco propter insula est
teretique forma caespes editur salo.
605　in continenti et inter adsurgentium
capita iugorum rursum harenosi soli
terga explica(n)tur seque fu(n)dunt lit[t]ora
orba incolarum. Setius inde mons tumet
procerus arcem et pinifer. Setii iugum
610　radice fusa in usqueTaurum pertinet
Taurum paludem namque gentici vocant
Orani propinquam flumini. huius alveo
Hibera tellus adque Ligyes asperi
intersecantur. hic sat angusti laris
615　tenui[s]que censu civitas Polygium est.
tum Mansa viscus oppidumque Naustalo
et urbs (impendet) + haesic(a)e gen(tis) salo
. . . .
. . . .
620　. . . . .
eiusque in aequor Cassius amnis influit.
at Cimenice regio disce[n]dit procul
salso ab fluento, fusa multo caespite
et opaca silvis. *nominis por[h]o auctor (est)*
625　*mons dorsa silvis dorsa celsus.* huius imos aggeres
stringit fluento Rhodanus atque scrupeam
mol[l]e(m) imminentis interrat aequore.
Ligures ad undam semel interni maris
Setiena ab arce et rupe saxosi iugi
630　*procul extulere.* sed quasi exposcit locus
Rhodani *ut fluentum plenius tibi disseram.*
stili immorantis pater(e) tracta[tu], mi Probe
quippe amnis ortum, gurgitis lapsum vagi,

---

608 setyus 609 Setii O: fecyi 615 *del. O* 617 *suppl. Schulten*
salo *idem:* sale 623 *ad* 624 opaca *Schrader: a prisca* 626 flueudo 629
Secyena 631 in 632 pater tracta mi Probe O: tractatu improbe

with round shape. On the mainland and amid the peaks of rising ridges the backs of sandy land fold back and the uninhabited shores spread **(608)**.

Next mount Setius swells. It is lofty with its citadel and pine-bearing. The ridge of Setius with its spread base extends all the way to the Taurus. For the tribesmen call the swamp near the river Oranus, Taurus. The Hiberian land and harsh Ligurians are divided by its channel. Here is the rather small and unpopulated town Polygium. Then there are the village Mansa, the town Naustalo, and the city[3] . . . **(617).*** Into its sea the river Classius flows.+

But the region Cimenice recedes far from the salty tide. ⸸ It spreads over a large area and is thick with forests. But the meaning of the name is "mountain high in the back" **(625)**. Its lower hills the Rhone touches in its course and it wanders through the rocky mass of the mountain that looms over the sea. The Ligurians spread themselves to the shore of the inner sea from the citadel of Setiena and the cliff of the rock ridge **(630)**.

But the situation requires that I explain more fully to you the river Rhone. Bear, my Probus, with my dwelling on the rising of the river, the course of the water's wandering, what peoples' land it washes. And we will say what great advantage the river brings

---

*   I have not translated the fragment that appears in the last half of line 617. With Schulten's additions the text seems to speak of still another people, the "Haesican tribe."

\+   I have translated "Classius" because the Cassius (line 621) of Schulten's text is an error.

⸸   With line 622 Avienus begins the last major division of his book: the Rhone to Massilia. The passage extends to the end of the text as we have it, line 714.

3.   Three lines have been lost. cf. *ed. princeps* p. 117.

    quas iste gentis lambat unda[s] fluminis
635 *quantoque manet incolis compendio*
    et [h]ostiorum fabimur divortia.
    nivosum in auras erigunt Alpes iugum
    a solis ortu et arva Gallici soli
    intersecantur scrupeo fastigio
640 et anhela semper flabra tempestatibus.
    effusus ille et ore semet exigens
    hiantis antri vi truci sulcat sola
    aquarum in ortu et f[r]onte primo naviger
    at rupis illud erigentis se latus,
645 quod [d]edit amne(m), *gentici cognomina(n)t*
    solis columnam. *tanto enim fastigio*
    in usque celsa nubium subducitur,
    meri(di)anus sol ut (op)positu iugi
    conspicuus haut sit, cum relaturus diem
650 *septentrionum ac(c)esserit confinia.*
    scis nam fuisse eius modi sententiam
    Epicureorum: non (eum) occasu premi,
    nullos subire gurgites, numquam oc(c)uli,
    sed obire mundun, obliqua caeli currere,
655 *animare terras, alere lucis pabulo*
    convexa cuncta et invicem regionibus
    cer(tis) negari canididam Phoebi facem.
    resi. . . . .
    . . . .
660 . . . .
    . . . .
    meridianam *cum secuerit orbitam,*
    cum lumen axi Atlantico inclinaverit,
    ut in supremos ignem Hyperboreos agat,
665 *Achaemenioque semet ortui ferat,*

---

  634 Quis 636 Ft 638 soli O: sali 644 ad 645 edit amnem *Casaubonus*: dedit amne 650 accesserit O: acerserit 657 *add.* O 662 meridianum 665 Achaemenioque *Wernsdorf*: Ac hemonioco qua

to the natives and what are the divisions of its mouth **(636)**.

The Alps raise their snowy ridge up into the sky in the east, and the fields of Gallic soil are cut by its rocky height. Winds are always breathing storms **(640)**. The Rhone flows from here and raising itself up at its source cuts through a gaping cave with savage force. It is navigable at its first source and rising. But that side of the ridge that rises up and gives forth the river, the natives call the "Pillar of the Sun" **(646)**. For it rises up to the heavens with such great height that the southern sun is scarcely visible due to the constant barrier of the ridge when the sun goes to the north to bring back the day **(650)**. For you know that such was the view of the Epicureans.* The sun does not set, it does not sink into the waters, it is never hidden. Rather it goes around the world, it runs through the corners of the sky, it gives life to the land, it gives nourishment with the food of its light to all the recesses, but to certain regions in turn, the bright face of Phoebus is denied **(657)**[4]. . . When the sun cuts through the southern course and the light sinks on the Atlantic axis in order that the sun spread its fire to the furthermost Hyperboreans and bring itself back to the Achaemenian rising, it bends toward other sections of the sky cur-

---

*   Avienus ascribes this view to the Epicureans. In reality it is the Ionian conception of the earth and sun. It is remarkable that Avienus or his sources go back to an older and less tenable view of the earth. This view presumes the earth is a flat disc or platter floating in the ocean, and that the earth, not the sun, is the center of the universe. Greek scientists had arrived at the globality of the earth, and some of them to the heliocentric nature of our universe; but older, less adequate, ideas perdured,

4. Four lines have been lost. cf. *editio princeps* p. 118.

	discreta in aethrae flectitur curvo ambitu
	metamque transit. cumque nostro obtutui
	iuber negarit atra nox caelo ruit,
	caec(a)equ nostra protinus tenebrae tegunt.
670	dies a[t] illos clara tunc inluminat,
	septentrione qui superposito rigent.
	cum rursus umbra noctis arctoos habet,
	genus omne nostrum splendidum ducit diem.
	meat amnis aut(em a) fonte per Tylangios,
675	per Daliternos, per Clahilcorum sata
	Lemenicum et agrum—*dura sat vocabula*
	auremque primam, cuncta vulnerantia,
	sed non silenda tibimet ob studium tuum
	nostramque cura(m). panditur porr[h]o in decem
680	flexus recursu gurgitum. stagnum grave,
	plerique tradunt, inserit semet dehinc,
	vastam paludem, *quam vetus mos Graeciae*
	vocitavit Accion, (at)qu[a]e praecipites aquas
	stagni per aequor egerit. rursum effluus
685	ar[c]tansque sese fluminum ad forma(m), dehinc
	Atlanticos in gurgites, nostrum in mare
	et occidentem contuens, evolvitur
	patulasque harenas quinque sulcat [h]ostiis.
	Arelatus illic civitas attollitur,
690	Theline *vocata sub priore saeculo*
	Graio incolente. multa nos Rhodano super
	narrare longo res subegerunt stilo.
	at numquam in illud animus inclinabitur,
	Europam ut isto flumine et Libyam adseram
695	*disterminari.* Phileus hoc quamquam vetus

---

668 negarit atra *Klotz*: negari terra 671 Septentrionis 674 *add. Wernsdorf* 676 Lemenicum *C. Müller*: Tem—680 flexus *Opitz*: vexis (in) grave *Unger* 682 vastam *Klotz*: vasta in; vastam in *Pithou* 683 atque *Schrader*: quae 684 aequore gerit 685 ad formam *Hudson*: ae forma

ved course and passes the goal **(667)**. And when he denies bright light to our view, black night rushes from the sky, and murky darkness suddenly covers all in our area. But clear day then enlightens those who shiver exposed to the north wind. But again when shade of night possesses the north, all our race passes a splendid day **(673)**.

The river then flows from its source through the Tylangi, the Daliterni, the fields of the Clahilci and territory of the Lemenici.* These are rather harshsounding words and they all offend the ear at first, but they are not to be omitted both because of your eagerness and my scholarship. The river then bends ten times with the meandering of its waters **(680)**. Many report that a thick swamp then inserts itself, a vast morass which old custom of Greece called Accion. And the river moves the rapid waters through the surface of the swamp. Again narrowing itself to the form of a river, and facing toward the Atlantic waters, our sea, and the west, it pours forth and cuts the spreading sand with five mouths. Here the city of Arelatus rises up. In a former age it was called Theline by the Greek inhabitants **(690)**. Many considerations have compelled us to write extensively on the Rhone. But my mind will never be inclined to assert that Europe and Libya are divided by that river. Phileus,+ though an ancient author, would

---

*   "Lemenici" is based on an emendation for the *'editio princeps'* "Temenicum." C. Müller proposed this, looking, no doubt, to the more familiar *Lemannus*. Otherwise, with the possible exception of *Tylangi*, the names in lines 674-76 are very strange and unfamiliar. This did not escape the notice of Avienus.
+   Phileas is the correct form of the name.

>   *putasse dicat incolas. despectui*
>   *derisuique inscitia haec sit barbara*
>   *et compete(nte denotetur nomine).*
>   cursus car[i]nae biduo et binoctio est.
> 700   gens hinc Nearchi Bergineque civitas,
>   Salyes atroces, oppidum [priscumra] Mastrabalae
>   (priscum) paludis, terga celsum prominens,
>   quod incolentes Cecylistrium vocant,
>   Massilia et ipsa est, cuius urbis hic situs:
> 705   pro f(r)onte lit[t]us praeiacet, tenuis via
>   patet inter undas, latera gurges adluit,
>   stagnum [l]ambit urbem et unda lambit oppidum
>   laremque fusa civitas p(a)ene insula est,
>   sic aequor omne caespiti infu[n]dit manus.
> 710   labos at olim conditorum diligens
>   formam locorum et arva naturalia
>   evicit arte. siqua[e] prisca te iuva[n]t
>   haec in novel(l)a nominum deducere

* * *

---

698 *add. Wernsdorf* 701 *del. Voss* 702 *add. Voss* paludis *Voss*: paludes 705 *add.* O 706 Pater 707 *del. Heinsius* 709 omne: omni *Wernsdorf* 710 Labol at *Schulten*: et 712 *del. Heinsius del. Schrader*
RUFI FESTI AVIENII OPERA FINIUNT

say that the inhabitants had thought this. Let this barbarous ignorance be despised and derided and branded with suitable name. The length of the journey for a boat is two days and two nights **(699)**.

Next is the tribe Nearchi and the city Bergine, the fierce Salyes, and the ancient town on the Mastrabalan lagoon, a promontory with lofty back, which the natives call Cecylistrium. Then there is Massilia itsell The site of this city is as follows. The shore stretches in front of it. A narrow entrance way opens between the waves. The swell washes its sides. A lagoon surrounds the city and the wave laps the town. As the city spreads its habitation, it is almost an island. So does the entire sea spread its force on the land **(709)**. But the careful labor of its ancient founders skillfully conquered the shape of the place and the natural fields. If you wish to reduce any of these ancient names to the new ones.*

* * *

---

* The text of Pisanus' edition breaks off at this point, but not much of the first book has been lost.

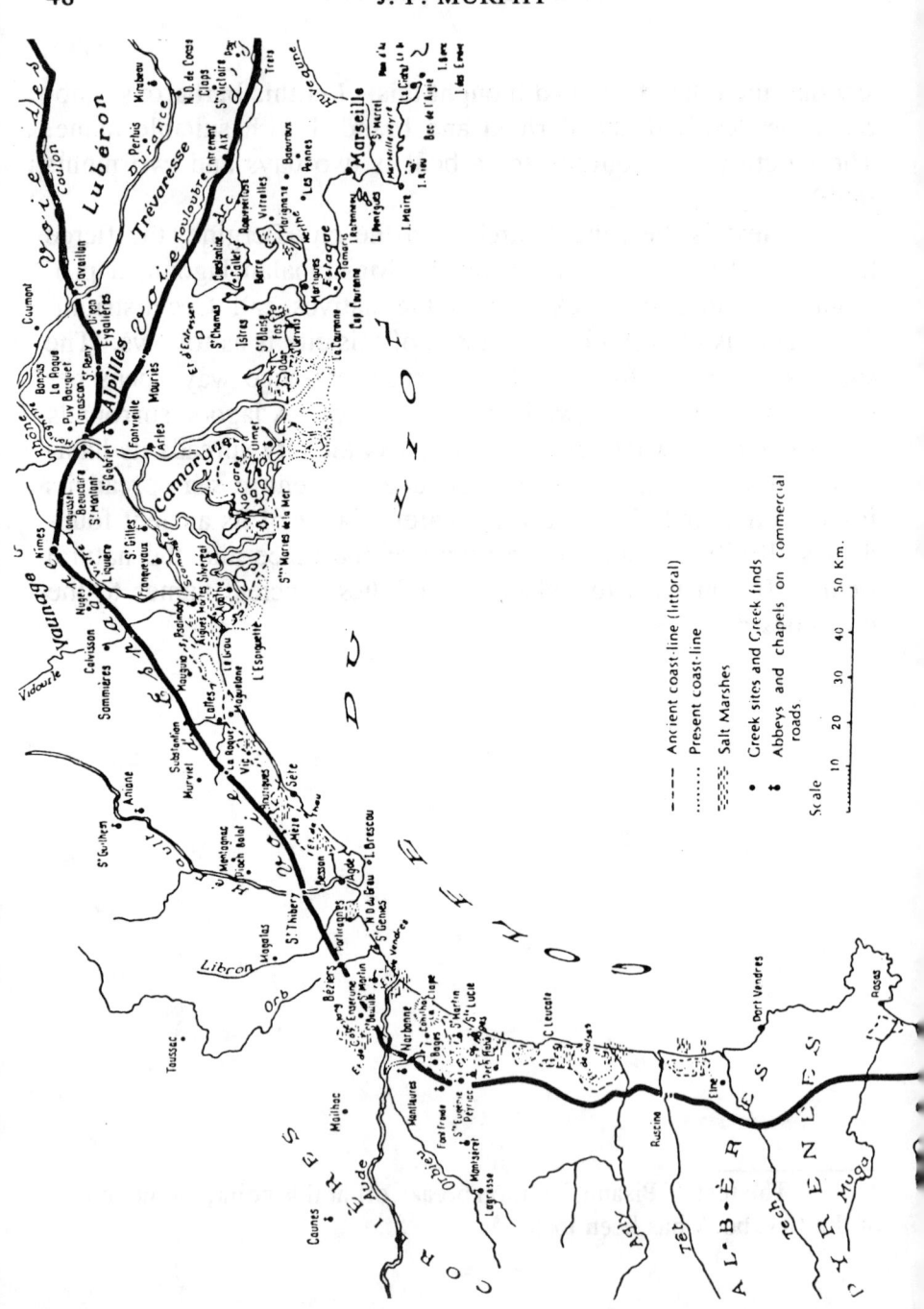

Commentary

I. Lines 10‑79: Exordium

A. Lines 10‑31: Address to Probus.

1. *Probe:* Schulten identifies this Probus as Anicius Petronius Probus (cons. 406 A.D.). Seeck, however, identifies him as Sextus Petronius Probus (born c. 330 A.D.-c. 390 A.D.; cons. 371 A.D.), the father of Schulten's choice. See *RE* 1, coll. 2205-07, *s. v.* Anicius #45 and #48. Marx (*RE* 2, col. 2289; *s. v.* Avienus #3) agrees with Seeck.

2. *Tautici ponti...situs*: This stands for the area of the Pontus and the Crimea.

9. *vetustis paginis*: This is the first of many references to an ancient document that lies behind Avienus' text. Cf. also *secretiore lectione* (line 11), *veterum abdita* (line 17), and *secreta rerum* (line 22). Fourth century authors had an exaggerated regard for ancient writers and are characterized by an archaizing trend. Although all commentators on Avienus do not agree with Schulten's sixth century B.C. date for the *Periplus*, they all admit very ancient material was used.

B. Lines 32-50. Aveinus' Sources.

32-33: *Maeotici...aequoris*: Sea of Azov.

33: *Sallustium*: B. Maurenbrecker (*C. Sallusti Crispi Historiarum Reliquiae*, Leipzig, 1891) has gathered the fragments of Sallust's *Situs Ponti* on pages 134-38.

42: *Hecataeus:* As indicated in the Prenote, the authors cited are probably taken from Ephorus. Hecataeus, of course, is the famous Ionian geographer and the only author cited who belongs to the sixth century B.C. The others are fifth century B.C. writers.

43: *Hellanicus*: Hellanicus was a fifth century B.C. historian and geographer from Mytilene.

43: *Phileus*: Phileas is the proper form of the name. He was from Athens and only 13 fragments have come down to us. In lines 691-96, Avienus preserves one.

44: *Scylax*: This explorer and geographer from Caryanda worked in the reign of Darius. The *Periplus* that is extant under his name is a fourth century B.C. document.

45: *Pausimachus*: Pausimachus is an unknown geographer from Samos. F. Gisinger (*RE* 18, 2.3, cot. 2433) raises questions about his work, including the possibility that he knew the West.

46: *Damastus*: Damastes is the correct form. He was a contemporary of Herodotus and based his *Periplus* on Hecataeus. Other sources state that he was from Sigeum. Sige is sometimes identified with Sigeum, at other times stated to be a port of Sigeum. Cf. Burchner *RE* 2A, col. 2276.

47: *Bacoris:* Like Pausimachus, Bacoris is unknown. He is mentioned only here.

47: *Euctemon*: Euctemon was an Athenian astronomer, meteorologist, and geographer. We learn of Euctemon's geographical work from Avienus, lines 336-40, 350-60, and 375-80.

48. *Cleon*: Although Cleon is cited several times by ancient writers, little is known of him.

50: *Thucydides*: The citation of Thucydides as *decus loquendi* was one of the indications which convinced Schulten that the Greek interpolator should be dated in the first century B.C., when the Atticist-Asianic debate raged.

C. Lines 51-79: The Scope of Avienus' Work.

51-73: Avienus mentions islands, bays, promontories, cities, major rivers (the Tartessus and the Rhone), ordinary rivers, islands in rivers, ports, swamps, lakes, mountains, and forests. The word *stagnum* presents a problem for the translator. Sometimes it means "swamp." At other times it signifies "lagoon." In still other passages, it means part of the sea separated from the main body by a strip of land (Italian: *lido*). These last places were important for sailors because they afforded shelter in storms.

54: *freto Tartessio*: Tartessus is an old name coming from the Phocaeans. Schulten (*Tartessos*, pp. 12-14) derived the name ultimately from Tursa in Lydia. Rhys Carpenter (*Beyond the Pillars of Hercules*, (pp. 59-60) sees a memory of this ancient name in Livy's *Tertis*. "This (Tertis) was the non-Greek and non-Phoenician word that the Greeks Hellenized into 'Tartessos' and the Carthaginians identified with a Semitic word already familiar to them 'Tarshish'. The name *fretum Tartessium* seems to be very old and refers to the Gulf of Huelva.

72: *illo volumine:* Avienus refers to his adaptation of Dionysius Perigetes in the *Descriptio Orbis Terrae*.

II. Lines 80-171: Northern and Western Seas.

85: *dicta Tartessus prius*: Schulten is convinced that the interpolator made an incorrect identification of Tartessus with Gadir/Gades. In Schulten's mind it was a frequent error among the ancients.

86: *columnae*: The *Periplus* began with the Northern Pillars (*duro perstrepunt septentrione,* lines 88-89). The interpolator confused this with the well-known Pillars of Hercules. The correct identification of the Northern Pillars seems to be Ouessant, the extreme part of the peninsula of Brittany. Formerly it was a cape, now Ouessant is an island. In his edition of Avienus (Paris, 1934), Berthelot (p. 57) maintains that the text does, in fact, refer to the Pillars of Hercules and that the north wind is mentioned because the Romans had a false orientation of the southern coast of Spain. They thought it ran directly east to west.

91: *Oestrymnin*: The Northern Pillars was the poetic name, *Oestrymnis iugum* the actual one. The name is derived from the people called *Oestrymnides* (line 113) or *Oestrymnici* (line 155). The *Periplus* distorted the name by deriving it from οἶστρος. Pytheas called them Οἰστρύμνιοι (*Apud.* Strab. 3. 63, 64, and 195). Later forms were 'Ωστίωνες and Ossismi. The name appears to be Ligurian. Carpenter (*Beyond*, p. 202 and 205) identifies Oestrymnis with Pointe du Raz, which is a promontory farther down the coast. In his commentary and translation of Avienus' *Ora Maritima* (Darmstadt, 1968), Dietrich Stichtenoth elaborated his theory that the *Periplus* dealt with the northern seas. Thus for him Oestrymnis was southern Sweden. He also made such identifications as Rhodanus-Oder, Gadir-on the delta of the Oder, Pillars-straits between Denmark and Sweden. Needless to say, his views have not been met with acceptance.

95: *sinus ... Oestrymnicus:* This is the gulf between the cities of Brest and Douarnenez. It is called the Bay of Douarnenez.

96: *insulae... Oestrymnides*: Schulten identifies these as the little islands scattered to the east of Ouessant. Carpenter states these islands were not themselves rich in metals, but served as markets for trade (*Beyond*, p. 205). Arribas concludes from this passage that the Tartessians were the first to use the Atlantic tin route and that the tin trade was one of the sources of its prosperity (*The Iberians*, pp. 49-50). Berthelot (p. 58) located these islands off the southwest coast of Britain. This identification has not been accepted.

108: *sacrum ... insulam:* Ireland. This is a translation of the Ionic ἱερὴ νῆσος. The native name was Hierne (Carpenter: (Hi(v)eiryo). The entire section deals with the navigation of the Oestrymnici in the northern sea. The Oestrymnici told the Tartessians of these areas, and they, in turn, recounted the tales to the Massiliotes. Specifically Irish products discovered in southwestern Spain confirm this trade between Tartessus and Ireland (see H. N. Savory, *Spain and Portugal*, p. 233).

111: *insula ... Albionum*: Albiones is a pre-Celtic name, probably Ligurian. Avienus is speaking of Britain here. Berthelot (p. 58) locates the land of the Albiones in Scotland.

114-129: Since the Carthaginians are mentioned, Schulten considers this passage to be from the interpolator's pen. Carpenter (*Beyond*, pp. 212-214) examines the voyage of Himilco, but cannot decide exactly where he explored. Carpenter notes that lines 122-24 have reminded commentators on Avienus of the Sargasso Sea, a great tract of floating seaweed in the mid-Atlantic. He doubts, however, that Himilco could have ventured that far out. The horrors of the Ocean, as recounted by Himilco, are repeated in lines 383-414. This is the sole passage preserved from Himilco's work.

129-145: The Oestrymnici explored north and east of Brittany, the area later inhabited by the Frisians. Thus they sailed through the Straits of Calais. Carpenter, however, argues that Avienus' *axe qua Lycaonis rigescit aethra* should be taken literally as northward, and not north and east as Schulten does. For Carpenter, Avienus is speaking of a struggle in Caledonia, modern Scotland. (*Beyond*, pp. 208-09). Berthelot (p. 59) agrees with Schulten's general orientation, but locates *the caespitem Ligurum* farther north in Jutland, modern Denmark.

131-32: *Lycaonis aethra*: This means the north. Lycaon was the father of Callisto, who, in turn, was identified with Arctos, the constellation of the northern sky. Ovid used this same mythological allusion in *Tristia* II. 2.1-2: *Ergo erat in fatis Scythiam quoque visere nostris/quaeque Lycaonis terra sub axe facet.*

132: Schulten accepts this evidence of the Massiliote *Periplus* that Ligurians once dwelled this far north. The invasion of the Celts from Scandanavia and the defeat of the Ligurians must have been completed by the seventh century B.C. Schulten identifies the mountains in which the Ligurians took refuge as the Alps.

145: *marinos locos:* These would be the shores beneath the maritime Alps.

146: *post ilia*: The *Periplus* returns to the point of its excursus, Oestrymnis and the Oestrymnic Islands.

147: *magnus . . . sinus*: This is the great bay extending from Oestrymnis to Ophiussa. Later it was called the *sinus Aquitanicus,* today the Bay of Biscay.

147: *Ophiussam:* This word means "Land of the Serpents" and stands for Spain here. The -οῦσσα ending indicates the Phocaean origin of the name.

148-51: Schulten conjectures that this land passage was opened by the Massiliotes since Carthage had closed the sea route. This seems to be too short a time for the long trip of 400 kilometers, but could be done in the long days of summer and with frequent change of horses.

154-57: These verses are the source for the older name of Spain, Oestrymnis, and the newer one, Ophiussa. That Oestrymnis is used both for Spain and Brittany is explained by the Ligurians' migration northward from the south (Africa?) via northwestern Spain. Schulten sees a kernel of historical truth in the rout of the Oestrymnici by serpents in that the Sefes-Ceits were called σῆπες and their totem was a snake. Arribas (*The Iberians*, p. 3) summed up Schulten's theory on the early peoples of Spain: "He postulated a native Ligurian population on which were superimposed the Iberians from Africa and the Celts from Central and Western Europe." But present opinion is that the Ligurians never reached the Iberian peninsula (*ibid.*, p. 22), but some still hold out for the presence of Ligurians there.

158: *Veneris iugum:* This is Cape Higuer, the westernmost cape of the Pyrenees. Berthelot locates all these geographical sites farther west (p. 67).

159: *insulas duas*: The two islands in question are Los Briquets and Amuiz.

160-61: *Aryium . . . prominens*: Cape Ortegal. Schulten feels the better spelling is Ambian since the name seems to come from a Celtic tribe, the Arubii. Berthelot (p. 67) identified it with Cape Silleiro.

164-65: *insula . . . Saturno sacra*: Berlenga. It is called *pelagia* since, in contrast to other islands cited, it is far off shore. Today it still abounds in grass. The *Saturnus* mentioned here and in lines 215-16, Schulten considers to be Phoenician Baal.

III. Lines 171-261: Western Sea, Ophiussa to Tartessus.

171-72: *prominens . . . Ophiussae*: Cape Roca, the westernmost point continental Europe. It is also the last name in -οῦσσα, and thus marks the

Phocaeans' farthest advance, From this point on the treatment becomes much more detailed.

174: *sinus:* Avienus is describing the Bay of Lisbon.

178: *si petat quisquam pede*: The land route was opened up for trade purposes after the Carthaginians gained control of the Straits of Gibraltar. Schulten sees in lines 178-82 an important notice from the last days of Tartessus before its destruction by the Carthaginians.

182-82: *Cempsicum iugum:* Cape Espichel.

184: *Achale*: Costa da Gale. Today it is a peninsula.

187-94: The phenomenon described here by Avienus is due to the river Sado that darkens the sea water with its mud.

195-96: *Cempsi atque Sefes*: According to Schulten, these were Celtic tribes that occupied the valleys of the Duero, Tajo, and Anas. This view has not met with general acceptance. Most hold that the Atlantic seaboard was held by tribes that are more likely to be pre-Celtic than Celtic (see Savory, *Spain and Portugal* p. 239).

197: *Draganum:* For Schulten, this is a Ligurian tribe that occupied northern Spain, the area later inhabited by the Gailaeci, Cantabri, and the Astures.

199-200: *Poetanion ... patulus portus*: The port is the mouth of the river Sado; Poetanium, now a peninsula, is in front of the city Setúbal. Berthelot (p. 70) thinks Poetanium is the island Percebeira.

201: *populi Cynetum*: Schulten believes the Cynetes were a Ligurian people driven from the area around Coimbra to the south and east.

201: *Cyneticum iugum*: Cape Saint Vincent. Most ancient authors called it Sacred Cape from a shrine on it, dedicated, in Schulten's opinion to Saturnus (= Phoenician Baal).

202: *qua ... est*: That is, in the west.

203: *Europae extimum*: The *Periplus* is in error to think that the *Cyneticum iugum* (Cape St. Vincent) is the farthest point of Europe. The confusion with Cape Roca (*prominens Ophiussae* in the text, lines 171-72) may be due to the fact that both places were popularly known as "Sacred Cape."

205-11: Avienus skips ahead to described the eastern boundary of Cynetes, the river Anas (today, the Guadiana). Properly its description should come after line 240.

206: *sinus*: In line 424, the bay is modified by the adjective *Calaticus*. Today its name is Huelva.

212-13: *insularum duarum*: The smaller island which lacked an ancient name is called today Leixâo. The modern name of Agonis is Armação. There is also a third, tiny island today called Caixâo. Berthelot (p. 74) locates Agonis farther west and identifies it with Baretta, which is also called dos Caes.

215: *cautes sacra Saturni et ipsa:* Cape Sagres. Berthelot suggests that it is the cape that moderns call Santa Maria (p. 75).

220: Avienus writes an adaptation of Vergil, *Georgics* 3.312: "*usum in castrorum et miseris velamina nautis.*"

225-26: *iugum Zephyro sacratum:* This is an extensive mountain between the cities of Loule and Tavira. Thus the *arx Zephyris* would be Mount Figo

228-37: Today too, the area around the mouth of the Guadiana experiences overcast and humid weather.

241: *iugum . . . sacrum infemae deae*: This seems to be the hill on which today stands the monastery of Santa Maria de la Rábida.

243-44: *palus Erebea:* This is a take formed in the mouth of the Tinto. The Phocaeans located in this area the fabulous places connected with Tartarus. Thus *palus Erebea* and the city *Herbi* are etymologically connected with the Greek ’Ερεβος. Schulten conjectures that Herbi may have been the port city of Tartessus for the exportation of metal. It

248: *Hiberus ... amnis*: The Tinto.

251: *Vasconas*: This tribe became known to the Romans during the war with Sertorius. Hence Schulten places the date of the interpolator toward 70 B.C. See Sallust, *Hist.* frag. #93 (Maurenbrecher, pp. 99-100).

253: *Hiberiam:* This name preserves a memory of the first seat of the Iberian tribes that crossed over from Africa and then spread along the east coast of Spain toward the Rhone. Berthelot (p. 78) feels this passage is too frail a basis to support a theory of an African origin for the Iberians.

254: *Tartessios et Cilbicenos:* On these peoples, see lines 295-303.

255: *Cartare ... insula*: This is the island formed by the two branches of the Tartessus river. Today there is only one mouth, but Strabo (3.140), Pausanias (6.19.3), and Ptolemy (2.4.4) attest to the existence of two in antiquity.

257: The Cempsi were routed from Cartare by the Tartessians.

259: *Cassius. . . mons:* Cerro de Asperillo. Avienus derives the name from the Greek κασσίτερος, but Schulten feels that the Greeks transferred the name from a dune of that same name in Egypt.

IV. Lines 261-317: Tartessus and Environs.

261: *fani . . . prominens:* The promontory of the temple would be on the north side of the mouth of the Baetis.

263: *Gerontis arx*: The citadel of Geron would be on the south side of the Baetis' mouth. Schulten proposes that it was on the reef Banco de Salmedina.

265: *sinus Tartessii*: This is the ancient, southern mouth of the Baetis.

269: *Tartessus:* Adolph Schulten spent many years in trying to prove the location of Tartessus on the south branch of the Baetis. He believed he found it in front of the city of Bonanza, at a spot called "La Marismilla," Founded in 1100 B.C. and flourishing till its domination by the Phoenicians, it experienced renewed prosperity in the period 700-500 B.C. It is often identified with biblical Tarshish. If, indeed, it did exist as a city, it was the oldest commercial and industrial center of the West. Carpenter argued strongly against identifying Tartessus with biblical Tarshish (*Beyond*, pp. 60-61). He also contradicts Schulten as to the existence of Tartessus as a city. At most it was a string of villages along the Tartessus River. Thus for Carpenter, Schulten's search was in vain. More recent opinion has swung back to Schulten's view that such a city or territory did exist (Arribas, *The Iberians*, p. 29). Berthelot also questions the existence of Tartessus as a city and feels the Tartessians' capital would have been at Seville (pp. 80-82).

266: *dictoque ab amni:* This should refer to the Anas in line 205, the last place where Avienus reported sailing time (line 222).

267-83: The interpolator confused Tartessus with Gades, which was a common error in antiquity. The interpolator also added the etymology of the name, which is characteristic of him. Cf. lines 260, 345, 624.

270-72: Schulten assigns the contrasts between ancient glory and recent ruin to Avienus. Marx (*RE* 2, col. 2388) holds Avienus was proconsul in Baetica, and thus had the opportunity for first hand observation (Line 274: *vidimus miri nihil*). Avienus himself tells us that he was twice proconsul (C.I.L. VI.1, nr. 537: *gemino proconsulis auctus honor[e]*). Another inscription (I.G. ii/iii 3(i) 4222) is commonly used to determine one of these proconsuiships as that of Achaea. Marx' assignation of Bactica as the second is, as we have seen, an inference from line 274. More recently J. Matthews (*Historia* 16 (1967), p. 489) has denied the existence of a proconsuiship of Bactica in the fourth century and uses a recently discovered inscription from Bulla Regis to propose Africa as the province for Avienus' second proconsulship. The form of the name in the inscription is Postumus Rufius Festus Abienius, which, to my mind, renders the assignation tenuous. A. Cameron, however, agrees with Matthews (*CQ* 18 [1967] p. 392).

275-83: Schulten conjectures that Avienus saw an inscription at Gades that commemorated Juba's duumvirate and hence he added this notice.

283: *insulam:* sc. Cartare.

284: *ex Ligustino lacu:* This "lake" would be the lagoon below the city of Coria. For Schulten, the name comes from the Ligurians who once held all of Spain. Others hold that this is the only evidence of the Ligurians' presence at the mouth of the Baetis and suggest emendations of the text that would connect the word with Libya (see Berthelot, p. 86).

288-89: The determination of the seven mouths of the river is very difficult, especially for the four mouths in the south. Schulten thinks these latter were caused by three alluvial islands in the river's mouth. Today there is only one island.

291: *mons . . . Argentarius:* This mountain is not near the *locus Ligustinus*, but at the river's source near the city of Cá.stulo. Since the Phocaeans sailed the coasts, they did not have personal knowledge of the interior. Perhaps the mountain is Cerro de San Cristóbal.

300: *gens Etmaneum:* This is the only place in which this tribe is mentioned.

302: *Ileates:* Strabo, citing Asclepiades (3.166), refers to this people as Ἰυῆτες.

303: *Cilbiceni*: This is a Tyrian name, transplanted from Lydia as are the city Cilpe and the river Cilbus.

308: *Tartessiorum* mons: This would be the hills between Cádiz and Sanlúcar.

309: *Erythia:* Erythia was added by the interpolator and seems to be the island of Gades. It is noteworthy that Gades is bypassed by the *Periplus*. It and other Phoenician cities such as Malaca, Sexi, and Abdera are omitted because of the hatred of the Phocaeans for their rivals, the Phoenicians and Carthaginians. Carpenter identifies Erythia as Isla de Leon, which is a little farther south than where Schulten would locate it (*Beyond,* p. 59).

315: *Veneii marinae . . . insula:* The little island of San Sebastian, which today is joined to the big island of Cadiz. It is noteworthy that the *Periplus* mentions this minor local shrine, but not the famous one of Hercules at Gades. This is another indication of animosity toward Carthage.

V. Lines 317-342: Spanish Coast from Tartessus to Cape Nao.

320: *Besilus atque Cilbus*: The Barbate and the Salado de Conil. The Cilbus, though farther north than the Besilus, is listed second for metrical reasons.

322: *Sacrum ... iugum:* Mount Meca on Cape Trafalgar.

323: *Herma:* The shoals between Cape Trafalgar and Cape Espartel. Berthelot (pp. 89-90) locates the shoals to the west, between Cape St. Vincent and Cape Trafalgar.

337: *Amphipolis ... incola*: Elsewhere Euctemon is said to be an Athenian. He must have gone to Amphipolis at one time. Cf. Rehm, *RE* 6, coll. 1060-61.

341: *Herculanae ... columnae*: If this name is in the *Periplus,* it is the earliest mention of the Pillars of Hercules. Heretofore they were known as the *Columns of Atlas.*

347: In the *Asinaria,* line 11, Plautus equates barbarian with Latin: *Demophilus scripsit, Maccus vortit barbare.* This is an addition of Avienus.

349: The interpolator cites several authors, probably taken from Ephorus.

353: *insulas duas:* Near Europe there is the island de la Paloma; the other near Africa is Isla del Perejil. The islands are much more than thirty stades apart (5.5 kilometers). They are 16 kilometers apart.

364: *navigia onusta adire non valent.* Schulten explains this as a restriction placed on Greek merchantmen by the Carthaginians. They were allowed to sail to Noctiluca with cargo, but no farther. If they wanted to worship on the island in the Straits, they had to sail without cargo. A. Garcia y Bellido (*Hispania Graeca*, vol. II, p. 10) maintains that

367: *ad Lunae insulam:* As the previous note indicated, Schulten identified this island with the Noctiluca of line 429. Once again Garcia y Bellido disagrees. Berthelot (p. 90) thought it was Terifa.

the verses refer literally to the difficult sailing conditions around the island Sancti Petri, and rejects Schulten's explanation.

367: *ad Lunae insulam:* As the previous note indicated, Schulten identified this island with the Noctiluca of line 429. Once again Garcia y Bellido disagrees. Berthelot (p. 90) thought it was Terifa.

371: *stadia septem*: Damastes' figure does not differ much from Scylax', for the width of the Bosporus is four to seven stades. The minimum width of the Straits is 14 kilometers or 70 stades. Only after the defeat of Carthage by Rome were the geographers able to give more accurate information on the Straits of Gibraltar.

383-89; 406-413: The same horrors of the Ocean have already been described in lines 120-29.

390-405: Avienus rather ineptly introduces this excursus on the four major gulfs of the Ocean. His source is Dionysius Perigetes. The *Hespericus aestus atque Atlanticum salum* refer to the Mediterranean. Cf. also the *Descriptio Orbis Terrae,* lines 77-82.

419: *Chrysus*: The Guadiaro. The *Periplus*'name reflects the view that the river carried gold down with it. The native name of the river was Barbaesula (Pomponius Mela 2.94 and Ptolemy 2.4.7).

421: *Libyphoenices:* Phoenician colonists from Libya, The *Periplus* is the oldest witness of this name. He omits, however, their cities Abdera, Sexi, and Malaca.

422: *Massieni*: These were a great tribe that extended from the Chrysus to Mastia (Carthago Nova).

422: *Cilbicene:* This is Schulten's correction of the traditional reading *Selbyssina.*

424: *Calacticum sinum:* Bay of Huelva. The adjective comes from the Greek καλὴ ἀκτή.

425: *iugum Barbetium:* Cape Calaburras.

426: *Malachaeque:* The interpolator introduced this name and has confused Málaga with Menace. Menace was the Phocaeans' westernmost colony. Schulten believed he had found the site of Menace west of Torre del Mar and 27 kilometers east of Málaga. His excavations revealed the Greek colony of Menace to be on a hillock west of the Vélez. Garcia y Bellido urges caution in order not to go beyond the real evidence (*Hisp. Graeca,* vol. II, pp. 5, 18-19).

427: *flumen:* The only river in the area is the Vélez.

429: *Noctilucae:* In line 367 it was called *Lunae insula.* The Tartessians retained control of the island in order to maintain the worship of the moon. Garcia y Bellido, who disagrees on the identification of *Lunae insula* and Noctiluca, feels the latter was a free port off Menace.

433: *Silurus* mons: Sierra Nevada.

434: *vasta cautes:* This is Pityussa, the name of which is derived from the Greek πίτυς. In an analogous manner, today the place is called *Sabinal* from the pine trees.

437: *Veneris iugum:* It is so called because the Greeks identified the marine goddess with Aphrodite. It is the Cape of Gata.

438: *litus* recumbit: Gulf of Amería.

444: *Herma:* Tres Forcas, which was visible to the Greeks from the cape as they went up to worship. The interpolator confuses this Herma with the Herma of line 323.

445: *litus ... patet:* Gulf of Baria.

449: *Namnatius ... portus oppidum prope:* Port of Cartagena. The town Mastia first stood there. In the text (line 452) it is *urbs Massiena.* The form Mastia is found in Hecataeus and Polybius. It seems to have been destroyed by the Carthaginians after 237 B.C. when in its place they founded *Carthago Nova.*

452: *iugum Trete:* Cape Palos. Trete seems to be the Greek τρητή "perforated" or "pierced." It was called "perforated" because of four caverns that the cape has on its seaward side.

453: *Strongyle . . . insula:* Grosa. The name Strongyle is a common one and comes from the adjective στρογγύλη, "round."

455: *immensa ... palus:* Mar Menor.

456: *Theodorus:* This is the Greek form of the name Tader. Today it is the Segura.

460-63: The gulf between the capes of Palos and Nao is being described here. Mela (2.93) and Pliny (3.19) call it *sinus Ilicitanus*. Today it is called the Gulf of Alicante.

461: *tres insulae:* Schulten identifies these as Plana, Benidorm, and Ifach (Calpe). Thus *late* in the text means "over a long distance," and that amounts to more than 50 miles. Carpenter (*Greeks in Spain*, pp. 155-56) argues that *late* here means "far out from land" and that Avienus is referring to the Islas Planas, which are Tabarca, Nao, and the West Reef (=Schulten's Plana). The *Periplus* mentions neither Alonis nor Akra Leuke, Massiliote colonies in the area. From this omission, Schulten concludes that they were founded after the writing of the *Periplus*. Berthelot (p. 100) thinks the *tres insulae* may be the Balearic Islands.

462: *hic*: Schulten argues that this adverb should refer to Cape Nao, not to the three islands. Thus he conjectures that Cape Nao (Ferraria in Mela [2.92], Tenebrium in Ptolemy [2.6.16]) was left out, perhaps due to Avienus' error. Even at this, the *terminus of* the Tartessians' power should be advanced to the Júcar.

463: *Herna:* Unknown city situated near Cape Nao. In his *Tartessos* (p. 68), Schulten observed, "*Von den 30 Städten die der Periplus nennt, sind 20 völlig unbekannt, . . .*" The general area of these unknown cities can be determined, but often no vestiges of them have been found despite much effort on Schulten's part to find them. Berthelot finds verbal echoes of many of the ancient names in modern names without, however, going so far as to identify the two.

464: Schulten reorders the lines here and reads 469 immediately after 464, for the island Gymnesia (Ibiza) cannot be said to lie "at the bed of the Sicanus that flows by." Carpenter (*Greeks,* p. 145) argues that the *insederant* in line 464 reflects a past tense in the *Periplus* and that the Iberians had already routed the Gymnetes. Therefore line 469 can stand where it is since the old name lived on in that area. He would set the boundary of the Tartessians' territory not at the Júcar as Schulten does, but at Alicante.

466: *Alebus:* The Vinalapó.

VI. Lines 473-621: Cape Nao to the Rhone: Northeast Spain and Southern Gaul

472: *Hiberi*: The *Periplus* uses this term for the Iberian tribes that were not politically subjected to the Tartessians.

475: *Ilerda:* This place seems to be where Jávea is today. The tribe Ilergetes or Ilercavones founded it, but later migrated and founded another Ilerda, which became modern Lerida.

476: *Hemeroscopium:* A colony of the Phocaeans, which Schulten located at Denia, Carpenter at Ifach. Since there is no swamp near Denia Schulten takes *stagnum* to mean "sea" here. Gabriela Martín has recently supported Schulten's view, but the excellent location of Ifach renders Carpenter's identification more probable (see G. Martín: 'La *supesta colonia griega de Hemeroskopeion: Estudio arqueológico de la zona Denia-Jávea"* (Valencia, 1968) and *Dianium: Arqueologia Romana de Denia* (Valencia, 1970). P. Bosch-Gimpera states the case for Ifach well in *El poblamento antiguo y la formación de los pueblos de España,* pp. 209-10.

479: *Sicana civitus:* This city was located on Cape Cullera at the mouth of the Júcar. Schulten observes that he hunted in vain for traces of it.

481: *divortio*: Today the Júcar has but one mouth.

482: *Tyrius ... Tyrin:* The river Tyrius is the Turia. The city of Tyris ought to have stood near Valencia.

485: *Berybraces:* This was a Celtic tribe that did business through the river Turia's valley with the shore's inhabitants and Greek merchants.

489: *Crabasiae iugum:* The height of Saguntum. Berthelot (p. 106) locates it a bit farther north at Cape Oropesa.

491: *Onussae Cherronesi*: Peñón de Peñíscola. The name Onussa comes from the Greek ὄνος, and was applied to the shore between Saguntum and Peñíscola because of its similarity to a donkey's back, Cheronesus is, of course, "peninsula." Berthelot locates the place in the delta of the Ebro (p. 106).

492: *palus ... Naccararum:* Albufera de Valencia. This place is south of Saguntum, but through a slip was placed out of proper order. Berthelot finds the swamp in the area around the Ebro's delta and identifies it with modern Alfaques (p. 106).

494-95: *insula ... Minervae*: Palmar, which is still rich in olives.

495-97: *Hylactes, Hystra, Sarna*: These are cities which were located on the coast between Denia and the Ebro.

498: *Tyrichae:* Market city of the Ebro. Later it was called Dertosa, today Tertosa. Hiberus is the Ebro and the name was interpolated into the text.

504: *mons Sacer*: The Montsiá to the south of the river Ebro. For Berthelot, it would be Sierra de Balaguer (p. 107).

505: *Oleumque flumen:* The Ebro. The name seems to be a translation of the Greek 'Ελαῖος which, in turn, seems to be a corruption of the Iberian Elaisos.

507: *mons Sellus:* The Coll Alba to the north of the river.

509: *civitas Lebedontia:* This city is to be located around Ampolla. Its name indicates that it was a colony of Lebedos.

513: *Salauris oppidum:* The name is preserved in the city and cape Salou; consequently the city is to be looked for there. Yet Schulten's investigations failed to turn up any vestige of the town. Berthelot (p. 107) suggests Sitges as its site.

514: *Callipolis:* This is the Greek name for Tarragona. According to Schulten, Terraco was the city's Etruscan name, Cesse the Iberian.

520: *Barcilonum amoena sedes ditium:* This is an interpolation of Avienus, for Barcelona was not a flourishing city at the time of the *Periplus* nor in the first century B.C.

523: *Indigetes*: The better form is Indicetes as found in line 532. This people occupied the area between Barcelona and the Pyrenees. A whole series of coins from Ampurias bear the legend UNDICeSCeN. See Eduardo Ripoll, José Mariá Nuix, and Leandro Villaronga, "Las monedas partidas procedentes de las excavaciones de Emporion" in *Actas del I Congresso Nacional de Numismatica,* p. 77.

525: *iugum Celehanticum*: This seems to be Cape Bagur, the most striking point of the eastern Spanish shore. Lamboglia ("*Encore sur la fondation d'Ampurias*" in *Simposio Internacional de Colonizationes: Barcelona, 1971,* p. 106) identifies the *iugum Celebanticum* as the chain of costal mountains that ends at Montgrí and le Montgo. For Berthelot, it is Cape de Tossa (p. 108).

527: *Cypselam:* This city probably stood at the mouth of the river Ter in Schulten's opinion. Although it is a Greek name (κύψελα), Schulten still feels it is a corruption of an Iberian name. Garcia y Bellido, on the other hand, thinks its origin is Greek. He also lists some conjectures on the site of Cypsela: Plaza de Pals, San Feliu de Guixols, Fonollera (*Hisp. Graeca,* vol. I, p. 169). Excavations carried on at Ullastret in 1951 have prompted some to identify Cypsela with Ullastret (Arribas, *The Iberians,* pp. 53-54; 102-03); but this inland site, 14 kilometers from the sea and some distance from a slow, narrow river renders the ascription impossible. Lamboglia (in "*Encore ...*" pp. 105-08) reiterated his earlier opinion that Cypsela is to be identified with the Palaeopolis of Ampurias. Oikonomides used an inscription and coins to confirm Lamboglia's identification ("New Evidence Supporting the Identification of the City of Kypsela with Palaeopolis in Ampurias," *Antipolis* I.1 (1974), p. 9-16).

530: *maximo portus sinu:* Gulf of Rosas. Ampurias and Rosas are not mentioned, and hence were not yet founded at the time of the *Periplus'* composition.

533: *Pyrenae ... verticem:* See line 565.

535: *Malodes:* For Schulten, this seems to be Torroelia de Montgrí. Lamboglia writes of *mons Malodes .... ne peut que correspondre au Cabo Creus, à la fin de la plaine*" (*"Encore ..."*, p. 107). Berthelot (p. 110) identifies it with the *mons Iovis and scalae Hannibalis* of Mela. Today it is named Mongo. This mountain is in the same group as Schulten's Torroella.

536: *scopuli duo*: Schulten explains these as two islands called today "Medas." There are actually six in the group, but two are the major ones. They provide a haven for ships against the east wind. Lamboglia underlines that Schulten is accepting a sixteenth century integration here (*sco[puli duo]*) and that integration, *"ne peut plus être retenue comme valable: il suffit de compléter scopuli [magni] ou autre, et il reste seutement l'allusion à une côté rocheuse, telle que celle du Cap Creus, entre Rosas et Crebère* (*"Encore ..."*, p. 107). Berthelot (p. 111) feels the poet is referring to the two ports Cadaquès and Puerto de Selva de Mar.

544: *stagnum ... Toni*: Schulten holds that this is the interior part of the Gulf of Rosas. Today only a part remains and is called Estanque de Castellón. The mountains referred to in the lines are the Pyrenees. Lomboglia again has another interpretation: "... *stagnum Toni (étang de Tolon) qui existe encore maintenant près de Castellón de Ampurias,"* c'est-à-dire au nord d'Ampurias" (*"Encore.* p. 107).

545: *Tononitaeque ... rupis:* For Schulten, this is the hill and village of Castellón on the lagoon. Lamboglia concisely states, *"Le iugum Tononitae rupis est donc précisément la chaîne des Albères"* (*"Encore ..."*, p. 107). For Berthelot (p. 111) it is one of, if not the entirety of, mountains north of Rosas.

547: *Anystus amnis:* the Muga.

550: *Ceretes ... et Ausoceretes:* For Schulten, these are Ligurian tribes that once inhabited the Pyrenees. The name Ausoceretes suggests a mixing of the Ceretes with their neighbors, the Ausetani.

552-53: *Sordus ... populus*: This was a Ligurian or Iberian people who held the plain of Rosellón. In later times an invasion of the Gauls drove them further into the interior.

559: *Pyrene*: According to Schulten, the city was probably located at the site of Rosas. The word *latera* was interpolated into the line from a marginal note. The author of that note thought that the city Latera (today Lattes) was identical with ancient Pyrene. Other suggestions have been made: Cadaquès, Selva del Mar, Elna, Port Vendres (Garcia y Bellido, *Hisp. Graeca*, vol. 1, pp. 168-69). J. Hind recently identified Pyrene with Ampurias (*Rivista storica dell'antichità* II [1972]), but he argues *ex silentio* (Pyrene must be Ampurias since the latter is not mentioned in Avienus) and is not convincing.

562-65: Schulten believes that behind this confused notice lies the *Periplus'* statement that it was a seven day voyage from Tartessus to Pyrene. That fits well with the 7,000 stades between the two places.

565: *Pyrenaeum iugum:* Cape Béar near Port Vendres. Again Lamboglia would apply this term to the chain of the Albères.

566: *litoris Cynetici*: The plain of Rosellón.

567: *amnis Rhoscynus:* Greek authors called this river by names that resemble Rhoscynus. Mela (2.84) calls it the Tetis (variant: Telis) and Pliny (3.32) the Tecum (variant: Tetum). Today it is the Têt.

569: *stagnum hic palusque*: Étang de Leucate.

574: *Sordus amnis*: The Agly. Today it flows around the Étang de Leucate, and not through it.

575-76: In the lacuna the *Periplus* mentioned the *iugum Candidum*. The present name of it, Leucate, is derived from the Greek Λευκὴ ἀκτή.

577-82: As the text resumes, the gulf of Narbo is being described. The three islands are Clape, St. Martin, and Ste. Lucie. Berthelot roundly criticizes the "philologists" who speculate that Clape was once an island (pp. 113-20). But he too must postulate the filling up of water passages by alluvial deposits in order to find the seven islands mentioned in lines 581 and 584. Instead of Clape, Berthelot suggests that Gruissan was once an island.

583-86: *sinus alter*: Étang de Bages et de Sigean. The four islands are united to the mainland today, but their locations can be plotted. Berthelot suggests the following identifications: Aute, Planasse, Soulier, Oulons (p. 122).

586: *gens Elesycum:* This was a Ligurian tribe that served as mercenaries for the Carthaginians (Herodotus: 7.165).

587: *Naro civitas:* Naro is an older form of Narbo, which was the chief city of the Elesyces.

589: *amnis Attagus*: Today the name of this river is the Aude. At the time of the *Periplus,* the river disgorged at Narbo, which was on the coast. Today Narbo stands 12 kilometers inland.

590: *Heliceque ... palus*: Étang de Capestang.

591: *Besaram:* Besara is the older name of Baeterrae, today Béziers. Besara seems to be the Ligurian form of the name, while Baeterrae is Gallic.

592: *Heledus ... Orbus flumina*: The Libron and the Orb. Berthelot (p. 122), however, considers the Heledus to be the Liton, a torrent that flows into the Orb at Béziers.

595: *Thyrius*: Other names of this river are Turicus, Arauris, and Cirta. Today it is called the Hérault. Berthelot identifies the Thyrius as the Libron, and takes the corrupt Cinorus of line 596 as the Hérault (p. 122).

595-600: The text lost in the lacuna described Cape Agde opposite Cape Candidum. As 599-600 indicate, the cape provided protection from winds. Agathe, the Massiliote trading post, would not have been mentioned by the *Periplus* since it was founded after the *Periplus* was written.

600: *Alcyonae quies*: Since the kingfisher was believed to make its nest on the sea, the name came to be used proverbally for "peace and quiet."

602-03: *quod Candidum dixi vocari*: The text refers to the lacuna at lines 576-77.

603: *Blasco... insula:* Brescou.

608: *Setius ... mons*: The hill of the city of Sète.

610: *Taurum paludem*: Étang de Thau.

612: *Orani ... flumini*: The Lez. At the time of the *Periplus,* this river formed the boundary between the Iberians to its west, and the Ligurians to its east. Arribas (*The Iberians,* p. 21) makes the curious identification of the Oranus with the Rhone: "Avienus includes under the general term 'Iberians' all the peoples of the coast between the river Júcar and the Orano (which must be the Rhone)." Arribas may, however, simply be correcting Avienus on the boundaries of the Iberians. Berthelot thinks the Oranus is the Rhony, a tributary of the Vistre (p. 123) or possibly the little rivulet, the Pallas (p. 128). Jannoray (*Ensérune,* Paris, 1955) follows C. Jullian's identification of the Oranus with the Hérault (p. 378).

615: *Polygium*: This town is unknown. Berthelot thinks it might be Bouziques (p. 123).

616: *Mansa vicus oppidumque Naustalo.* These places are likewise unknown. If Mansa were a variant of Mesua (Mela 2.80), it should have been named earlier. Berthelot takes *vicus* as a proper name and sees an echo of it in moder Vic; Mansa (Masua on his map) is found in modern Méze. Naustalo may have left a remnant in Maguelonne (p. 123).

617-20: In the lacuna, the lost verses described the swamp Manguio.

621: *Classius amnis*: The Colason which empties into the Étang de Manguio.

Berthelot offers as an alternative identification the Colazou (p. 123). The spelling Cassius in Schulten's text is an error in printing.

VII. Lines 622-714. The Rhone to Massilia.

622: *Cimenice regio*: Having arrived at the area of the Rhone, the *Periplus* has a digression on the Cévennes mountains. The *Cimenice regio* is Mt. Cévennes and forms the western boundary of the Rhone valley.

626: *Rhodanus:* As the Tartessus river received a very full treatment (lines 283-303), so too the Rhone receives ample treatment (lines 625-88).

637: *Alpes:* The Alps form the eastern boundaries of the Rhone valley. The word Alps means high mountains. It is Ligurian in origin.

638: *Gallici soli*: Schulten considers this verse to be of extraordinary importance since it indicates that the Gauls had occupied the Alps by the sixth century before Christ. The Celts migrated southward in the seventh century. At the mouth of the Rhine they divided into two parts. One followed the occan's coast and arrived in Spain. The second followed the river valleys of the Meuse, Saône, and Rhone and arrived at the Alps and passed into Italy. The eastern group was distinguished from the western by the name "Gauls" if the phrase *Gallici soli* is genuinely from the *Periplus*, it is the earliest witness of the name Gaul.

640: The wind in question is the Mistrel (northeast) which does harm to Gallia Narbonensis.

642: *hiantis anti*: The glacier cavern in which the Rhone rises near the village of Gletsch.

646: *soles columnam*: The Damnastock, from the recesses of which the Rhone springs.

646-73: The interpolator inserts a passage on the "Epicurean" view of the sun's movement through the sky. In reality, the Ionians held what is described here.

662: *axi Atlantico*: The west.

665: *Achaemenioque ... ortui*: The east.

674: *Tylangios:* A Ligurian tribe that Caesar (*de bello Gall.* 1.5.4) calls Tulingi. They were neighbors of the Helvetii.

675: *Daliternos*: This was a tribe around the river Dala, which flows into the Rhone close to the village of Leuk.

675: *Clahilcorum:* This people is unknown.

676: *Lemenicum ... agrum:* The Lemenici dwelt around the shores of the *Lacus Lemannus* (or *Lemennus*), which is the modern Lake Geneva.

683: *Accion*: The *palus Accion* stood where today there is the "Plaine de Fourques" between Arles and Tarascon.

687: *occidentem contuens:* Fomerly the chief mouth of the Rhone was the western one.

688: *quinque ostiis*: While Timaeus (*apud Strabo* 3.183) and Posidonius (*apud Diodorum* 5.25) distinguished five mouths of the Rhone, ancient authors generally list only three.

690: *Theline*: According to Schulten, Theline appears to be a name of Ligurian origin, while Arelate is Gallic. The text, however, clearly states that it is a Greek name and Theline seems to be an example of the Greeks' making place names from resemblances to the body.

699: The journey referred to is one from Pyrene to the Rhone or to Massilia.

700: *gens ... Nearchi*: An unknown tribe. Since the Avatici later occupied the same area, the Nearchi may be a Ligurian tribe that was displaced by the Gauls.

700: *Bergine:* Named after Bergius, who with his brother fought against Hercules on the nearby plain called "La Crau." Bergine seems to be the modern Berre.

701: *Salyes:* The more common form of the name is Saluvii. They seem originally to have been Ligurian, but later were forced to mix with the conquering Gauls. In their territory, Massilia is found.

701: *oppidum Mastrabalae paludis:* Town of Malestrou, situated on the entrance to the lagoon of Berre. Jannoray (*Revue archéologique* 36 (1950): *"A propos d'Avienus, Ora Maritima, vers 701-02."* pp. 77-83) argues that the *editio princeps'* reading *oppidum Mastrabalae/priscum, paludes...* should be retained. Thus Avienus refers to an ancient city (frequently identified as Saint-Blaise) and to swamps near the shore (and not the Étang du Berre) before Cape Couronne.

703: *prominens ... Cecylistrium:* Cape Couronne.

705-06: *tenuis via:* The isthmus between the port La Joliette on the north and the Old Port on the south. The *frons* is the part facing the sea. The *latera* are the two ports.

714: The ending of the first book of the *Ora Maritima* is lost, but since it is likely that Massilia was its *terminus ad quem,* not much has been lost.

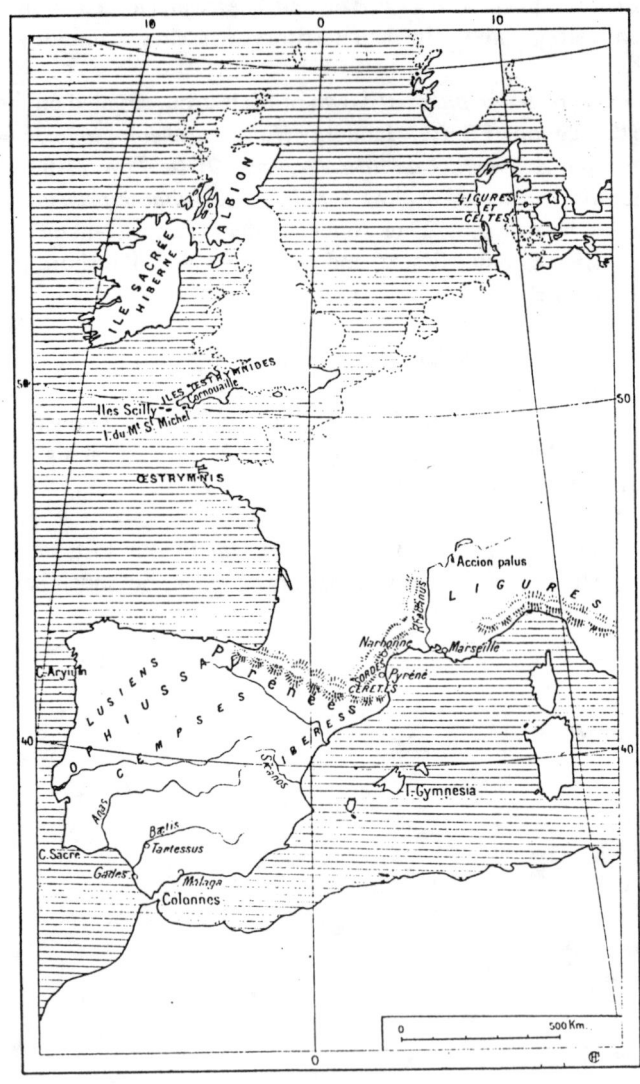

1. Western Europe according to Avienus (after Berthelot, p. 56)

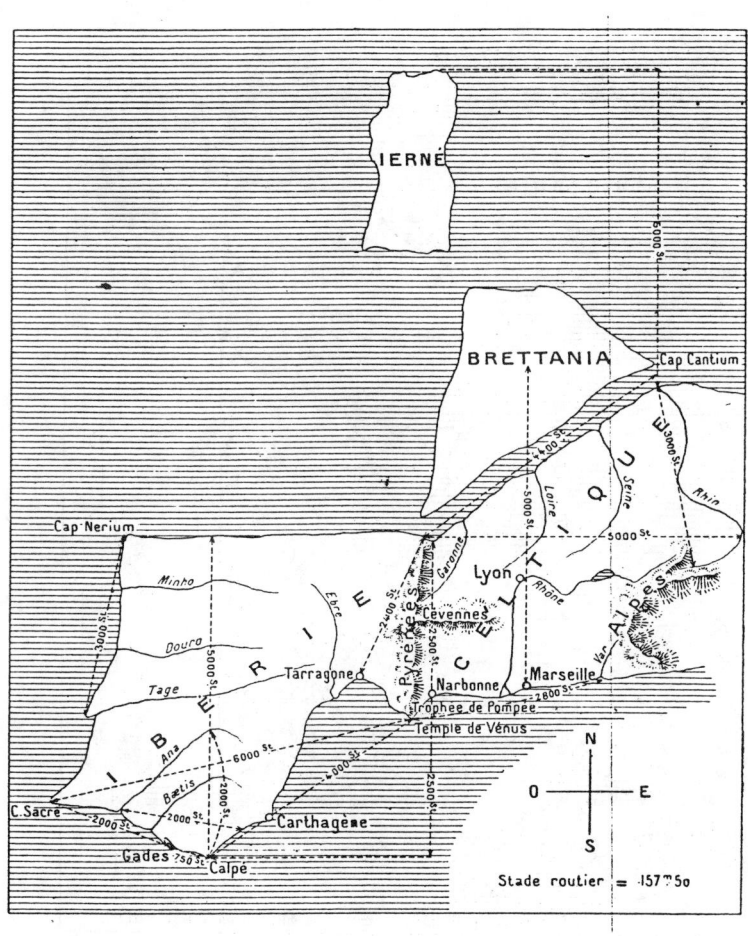

2. Western Europe according to Strabo (after Berthelot, p. 56a)

3. Western Europe according to Agrippa (after Berthelot, p. 56b)

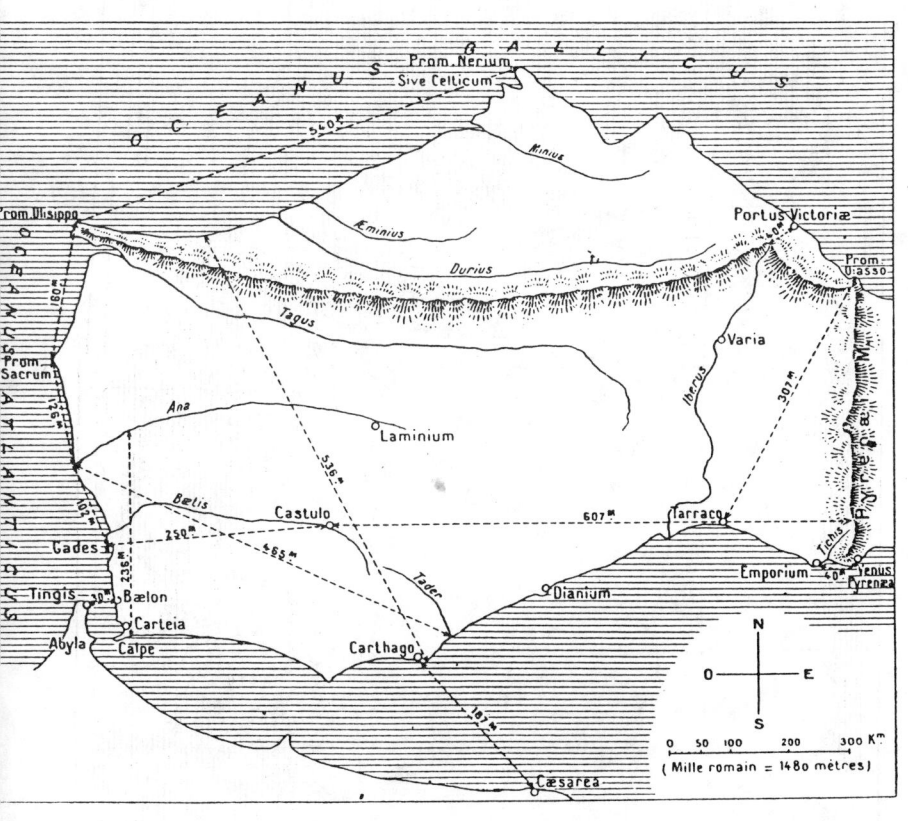

4. The Iberian Peninsula according to Agrippa (after Berthelot, p. 57)

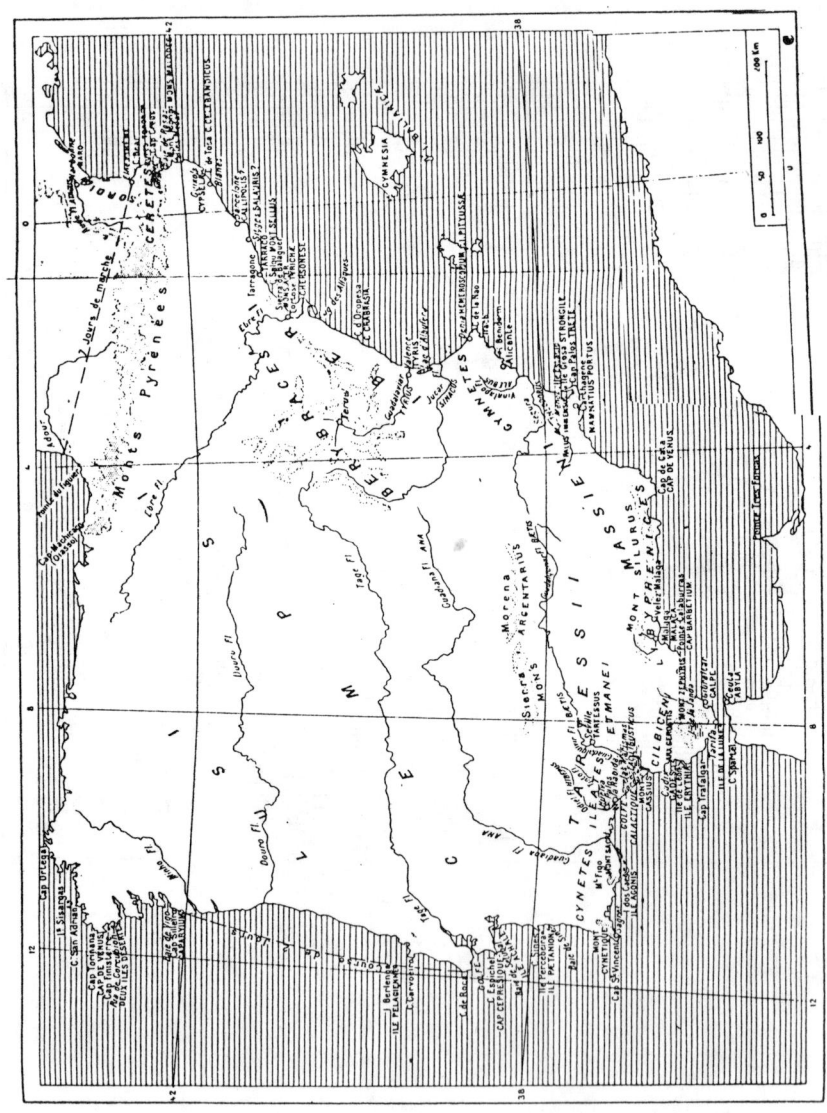

5. The Iberian Peninsula according to Avienus (after Berthelot, p. 64)

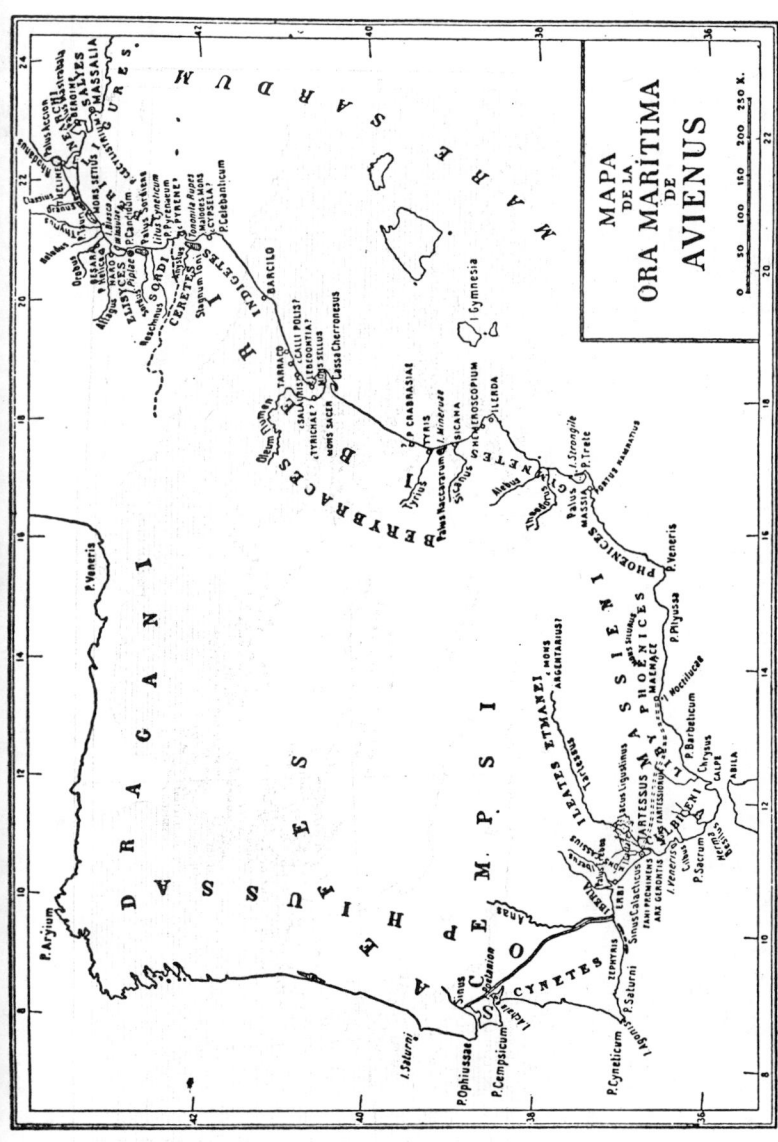

6. The Iberian Peninsula according to Avienus (after Schulten)

Select Bibliography*

Arribas, Antonio. *The Iberians.* New York, 1968.
Benoit, Fernand. *Recherches sur l'hellenisation de Midi de la Gaule.* Aix, 1965.
Blázquez, Joseé Mariá. "La colonización griega en España en el cuadro de la colonización griega en Occidente," in *Simposio Internacional de Colonizaciones: Barcelona, 1971,* edited by E. Ripoll Perelló and E. Sanmartí Grego. Barcelona, 1974. pp. 65-77.
_____. "Fuentes griegas y romanas referentes a Tartessos," in *Tartessos y sus Problemas.* Jerez de la Frontera, 1968. pp. 91-110.
Bosch-Gimpera, Pedro. *Palentologia de la Peninsula Iberica.* Graz, 1974.
Bunbury, E. H. *A History of Ancient Geography.* 2 vols. 2nd edition. New York, 1959 reprint of 1883 edition.
Burton, Harry E. *Discovery of the Ancient World.* Freeport, New York, 1969 reprint of 1932 edition.
Carpenter, Rhys. *Beyond the Pillars of Hercules: the Classical World Seen through the Eyes of its Discoverers.* New York, 1966.
_____. *The Greeks in Spain.* New York, 1971 reprint of 1925 edition.
Cuadrado, Emeterio. "Penetración de las influencias colonizadoras grecofenicias en el interior peninsular" in *Simposio Internacional de Colonizaciones: Barcelona, 1971,* edited by E. Ripoll Perelló and E. Sanmartí Grego. Barcelona, 1974. pp. 93-104.
Forbiger, Albert. *Handbuch der alten Geographie.* Graz, 1966 reprint (vol. 1: 1842; vol. 2: 1843; vol. 3: 1877).
Garcia y Bellido, Antonio. *Hispania Graeca.* 3 vols., Barcelona, 1948.
Gimeno, Mariá José Pena. "Artemis-Diana y algunas cuestiones en relación con su iconografía y su culto en Occidente," *Ampurias* 33 (1973) 109-34.
Gisinger, F. "Geographie" in Pauly-Wissowa's *RE Suppl.* IV.
Hind, J. "Pyrene and the Date of the Massaliot Sailing Manual," *Rivista storica dell'Antichità* 2 (1972), 39-52.
Jannoray, J. "A propos d'Avienus, *Ora Maritima,* vers 701-02," *Revue archéologique* 36 (1950) 77-83.

---

* For the editions of Avienus' *Ora Maritima* see p. X.

Lamboglia, Nino. "Encore sur la fondation d'Ampurias" in *Simposio Internacional de Colonizaciones: Barcelona, 1971*, edited by E. Ripoll Perelló and E. Sanmartí Grego. Barcelona, 1974. pp. 105-08.
Lentheric, Charles. *The Riviera: Ancient and Modern*. English translation by Charles West. Chicago, 1976 reprint of London 1885 edition.
Lot, Ferdinand. *La Gaule*. Revised edition by Paul-Marie Duval. Paris, 1967.
MacKendrick, Paul. *The Iberian Stones Speak*. New York, 1969.
Martín, G. *La supesta colonia griega de Hemeroskopeion: Estudio arqueológico de la zona Denia-Jávea*. Valencia, 1968.
_____. *Dianium: Arqueologia Romana de Denia*. Valencia, 1970.
Matthews, J. "Continuity in a Roman Family: the Rufii Festi of Voisinii," *Historia* 16 (1967) 484-509.
Oikonomides, Al. N. "New Evidence Supporting the Identification of the City of Kypsela with Palaeopolis in Ampurias," *Antipois* I.1 (1974) 8-16.
Powell, T. G. E. *The Celts*. London, 1958.
Properzio, Paul J. "Rhodian Colonization in Iberia: The Colony Rhode and the Townlet Rhodos," *Antipolis* 1.2 (1975) 83-96.
Savory, H. N. *Spain and Portugal*. New York, 1968.
Schulten, Adolph. "The Romans in Spain" *Cambridge Ancient History* VIII, Chapter 10.
_____. *Tartessos*. 2nd edition. Hamburg, 1950.
Sutherland, Carol H .V. *The Romans in Spain*. London, 1939.
Thomson, James Oliver. *History of Ancient Geography*. New York, 1965 reprint of 1948 edition.
Tozer, Henry F. *Classical Geography*. New York, 1885.
_____. *A History of Ancient Geography*. 2nd edition. New York, 1964.
Villard, François. *La Céramique grecque de Marseille (VIe-VIe siècle)*. Paris, 1960.
Villaronga, Leandro. *Las Monedas Hispano-Cartaginesas*. Barcelona, 1973.

Index of the Geographical Sites in Avienus' *Ora Maritima* and their Present Names[1]

Abila . . . . Ceuta
Accion palus . . . . Plaine de Fourques
Acer mons = Sacer mons
Achale insula . . . . Costa da Gale
Agonis insula . . . . Armaçâo
Albionum insula . . . . Britain
Alebus amnis . . . . Vinalapó
Alpes . . . . Alps
Ana amnis . . . . Guadiana
Anystus amnis . . . . Muga
Arabs gurges . . . . Arabian Gulf
Arelatus civitas . . . . Arles
Argentarius mons . . . . Cerro de San Cristóbal
Aryium iugum . . . . Cape Ortegal
Atlanticum Salum . . . . Mediterranean
Atlanticus sinus . . . . Bay of Cádiz
Attagus amnis . . . . Aude
Baliarium insularum . . . . Majorca and Minorca
Barbetium iugum . . . . Cape Calaburras
Barcilonum sedes . . . . near Barcelona
Bergine civitas . . . . Berre
Besara . . . . Béziers
Besilus flumen . . . . Barbate

---

[1] For the most part, I follow Schulten's identifications. The reader is referred to the commentary for a discussion of alternate sites suggested. Entries in boldface type are contained in the *Periplus;* those in ordinary type come from the interpolator or Avienus himself.

Blasco insula . . . . Brescou
Bosporus . . . . Strait of Constantinople
Callacticas sinus . . . . Gulf of Huelva
Callipolis . . . . Tarragona
Calpe . . . . Gibraltar
Candidam iugum . . . . Leucate
Canus see Sicanus
Cartare insula . . . . in mouth of Guadalquivir
Carthago . . . . near Tunis
Caspium mare . . . . Caspian Sea Cassae
see Onussa **Cassius** mons . . . . Cerro
de Asperillo cautes vasta (= Pityussa) . . . . Sabinal
Cecylistrium prominens . . . . Cape Couronne
Celebanticum iugum . . . . Cape Bagur
Cempsicum iugum . . . . Cape Espichel
Cepresicum see Cempsicum
Cherronesus see Onussa
Chrysus amnis . . . . Guadiaro
Cilbus flumen . . . . Salado de Conil
Cimenice regio . . . . area of Mt. Cevennes
Clahilcoram sata . . . . Unknown
Classius amnis . . . . Colason
Columna Solis . . . . Damnastock
columnae Herculis . . . . Gibraltar and Ceuta
Counmae Septentrionales . . . . Ouessant
Crabrasiae iugum . . . . Saguntum
Cyneticum iugum . . . . Cape St. Vincent
Cyneticum litus . . . . Plain of Roselló
Cypsela . . . . Palaeopolis in Ampurias
Erbi = Herbi
Erebea palus . . . . mouth of Tinto
Erythia . . . . island of Cádiz
Etrephaea see Erebea
Euxinum aequor . . . . Black Sea
Fani prominens . . . . north mouth of Guadalquivir
Fretum tenue (Line 335) . . . . Straits of Gibraltar
Gadir . . . . Cádiz
Gerontis arx . . . . Banco de Salmodina
Graecia . . . . Greece

Gymnesia insula	Ibiza
Heledus flumen	Libron
Helice palus	Étang de Capestang
Hemeroscopium	Ifach
Herbi civitas	near River Tinto
Herculanae columnae	Gibraltar and Ceuta
Herculis via = Herma	
Herma	between Cape Trafalgar and Cape Espartel
Herma (Lybiae)	Tres Forcas
Herna civitas	near Cape Nao
Hesperius aestus	Mediterranean
Hiberia	between Guadiana and Tinto
Hiberus amnis (line 248)	Tinto
Hiberus flumen (line 503)	Ebro
Hylactes civitas	Unknown
Hyrcana unda	Caspian Sea
Hystra civitas	Unknown
Iberus see Hiberus	
Ilerda civitas	Jávea (?)
Indiceticum litus	Gulf of Rosas
Indicorum salum	Persian Gulf
Infernae Deae iugum sacrum	near La Rabída
Insula Nominis Indiga (line 213)	Leixâo
Insula Sacra	Ireland
Insula Veneris Marinae	San Sebastian
Insulae Duae (line 159)	Los Briquets and Amuiz
Insulae Duae (line 353)	Isla de la Paloma and Isla del Perejil
Insulae Tres (line 461)	Plana, Benidorm, and Ifach
Insulue Tres (line 581)	Clape, St. Martin and Ste. Lucie
Lebedontia	near Ampolla
Lemenicus ager	near Lake Geneva
Libystidis columna = Abila	
Liguram caespes	West Friesland
Ligustinus lacus	below Coria
Litus recumbit (line 438)	Gulf of Almería
Lunae insula	at Ménaca
Maeoticum aequor	Sea of Azov
Malaca	Málaga
Malachae flumen	Vélez

Malodes mons	Torroella de Montgrí
Mansa vicus	Méze (?)
Massiena urbs	Cartagena
Massilia	Marseilles
Mastrabalae oppidum	Malestrou
Menace	west of Torre del Mar (?)
Minervae insula sacra	Palmar
Naccararum palus	Albufera de Valencia
Namnatius portus	port of Cartagena
Naro	Narbonne
Naustalo oppidum	Maguelonne (?)
Noctiluca	at Ménaca
Oestrymnicus sinus	Bay of Douarnenez
Oestrymnides insulae	east of Ouessant
Oestrymnis (line 154)	Spain
Oestrymnis iugum (line 91)	Ouessant
Oleam flumen	Ebro
Onussa Cherronesus	Peñón de Peñíscola
Ophiussa	Spain
Ophiussae prominens	Cape Roca
Ophiussae sinus (line 174)	Bay of Lisbon
Ophiussam, magnus sinus ad usque	Bay of Biscay
Oranus flumen	Lez
Orobus flumen	Orb
Palus Immensa (line 405)	Mar Menor
Patulus Portus (line 200)	mouth of Sado
Pelopis insula	Peloponnese
Persicus fluctus	Persian Gulf
Piplae	Aute, Planasse, Oulons, Soulier (?)
Pityussae insulae	Majorca and Minorca
Poetanion insula	in front of Setúbal
Polygium civitas	Bouziques (?)
Pyrenae (or **Pyrenaeum**) iugum	Cape Béar
Pyrene civitas	Rosas (?)
Rhodanus	Rhone
Rhoscynus amnis	Têt
Roschinus see Rhoscynus	
Sacer mons (line 504)	Montsiá
Sacra Insula	Ireland

Sacrum Iugum (line 322)	Mount Meca
Salauris oppidum	Salou (?)
Sardum aequor	Sardinian Sea
Sama civitas	Unknown
Saturni cautes sacra	Cape Sagres
Saturno insula sacra et pelagia	Berlenga
Sco[puli duo] (line 536)	Medas
Scythicum profundum	Black Sea
Selbyssina see Cilbicene	
Sellus mons	Coll Alba
Setiena arx	Sète
Setii iugum	Sète
Setius mons	Sète
Sicana civitas	on Cape Cullera
Sicanus amnis	Júcar
Silurus mons	Sierra Nevada
Solis Columna	Damnastock
Sordice palus	Étang de Leucate
Sordus amnis	Agly
Strongyle insula	Grosa
Tarraco	Tarragona
Tartessii sinus	mouth of Guadalquivir
Tartessiorum mons	between Cádiz and Sanlúcar
Tartessium fretum	Gulf of Huelva
Tartessius ager	valley of Guadalquivir
Tartessus	La Marismilla (?)
Tarrtessus amnis	Guadalquivir
Tauricus Pontus	Black Sea
Taurus palus	Étang de Thau
Theline	Arles
Theodorus amnis	Segura
Thyrius flumen	Hérault
Toni stagnum	Estanque de Castellón
Tononita rupes	Castellón
Traete see Trete	
Trete iugum	Cape Palos
Tyrichae	Tortosa
Tyris oppidum	near Valencia
Tyrius amnis	Turia

Veneris iugum (line 158)	Cape Higuer
Veneris iugum (line 437)	Cape Gata
Venah Marinae insula	San Sebastian
Zephyridis ora	between Loule and Tavira
Zephyris arx	Mount Figo
Zephyro iugum sacratum	between Loule and Tavira

Index of Proper Names[1]

Abdera 60, 61	Ampolia 66
Abila. . . . *lines 87, 88, 344, 345*	Ampurias 67, 68
Accion . . . . *line 682*, 72	Amuiz 54
Achaea 58	Anas . . . . *line 205*, 56, 58
Achale . . . . *line 184*, 55	Anicius 49
Africa 29n, 54, 57	Anystus . . . . *line 547*, 68
Agathe 70	Aphrodite 62
Agde 70	Aquitanicus sinus 53
Agly 69	Arabia 21n
Agonis . . . . *line 214*, 56	Arabs gurges . . . . *line 401*
Akra Leuke 63	Arauris 59
Alba, Coll 66	Arctos 53
Albères 68	Arelate . . . . *line 689*, 72
Albiones . . . . *line 112*, 52	Argentarius mons . . . *line 291*, 59
Albufera 65	Arles 72
Alcyon . . . . *line 600*, 70	Armaçâo 56
Alebus . . . . *line 466*, 64	Arribas, A . . . 52, 54, 58, 66, 70
Alfaques 65	Arubii 54
Alicante 46	Aryium prominens . . . *lines 160,*
Alicante, Gulf of 63	*172*, 54
Alonis 63	Asclepiades 59
Alps . . . . *line 637*, 53, 71	Asianic 50
Ameria, Gulf of 62	Asinaria 60
Amphipolis . . . . . . *line 337*, 60	Asperillo, Cerro de 57

[1]Numbers in Italics are the line numbers of Avienus' poem. The addition of the letter "n" means the item is to be found in the notes accompanying the English translation.

Assyria 21n
Astures 55
Atlanticum salum . *lines 398, 686,*
    viii, 61
Atlas, Columns of 60
Attagus . . . . *line 589*, 69
Atticist 50
Aude 69
Ausetani 68
Ausoceretes . . . . . . *line 550*, 68
Aute 69
Avatici 73
Avienus . . v, vi, vii, viii, ix, 3n,
    5n, 7n, 13n, 19n, 23n, 29n,
    31n, 39n, 41n, 43n, 49, 50,
    51, 52, 53, 57, 58, 59, 60,
    61, 63, 66, 68, 70, 73
Azov, Sea of 49
Baal 54, 56
Bacoris . . . . *line 47*, 50
Baeterrae 69
Baetica 58
Baetis . . . . ix, 57, 58, 59
Bages et de Sigean, Étang de . 69
Bagur 66
Balaguer, Sierra de 65
Baleares . . . . *line 471*, 63
Banco de Saimedina 58
Barbaesula 61
Barbate 60
Barbetium . . . . *line 425*, 62
Barcelona 66
Barcilones . . . . *line 520*, 66
Baretta 56
Baria, Gulf of 63
Béar, Cape 68
Benidorm 63
Bergine . . . . *line 700*, 73
Bergius 73
Berlenga 54

Berre 73
Berre, Étang du 73
Berthelot, A . . . . vi, vii, viii, ix,
    15n, 51, 52, 53, 54, 55, 56, 57,
    58, 59, 60, 61, 63, 65, 66, 67,
    68, 69, 70, 71
Berybraces . . . *line 485*, 33n, 65
Besara . . . . *line 591*, 69
Besilus . . . . *line 320*, 60
Beéziers 69
Biscay, Bay of 53
Blasco . . . . *line 603*, 70
Bonanza 58
Bosch-Gimpera, P 64
Bosporus . . . . *line 374*, 61
Bouziques 70
Brescou 70
Brest 52
Briquets, Los 54
Britain . . . . ix, 52
Brittany . . . . . . v, ix, 51, 53, 54
Bulla Regis 59
Burchner 50

Cadaquès 67, 68
Cádiz 59, 60
Caes, dos 56
Caesar 72
Caixâo 56
Calaburras 62
Calacticus . . . . *line 424*, 62
Calais, Straits of 53
Caledonia 53
Callipolis . . . . . *lines 514-15*, 66
Callisto 53
Calpe . . . . *lines 87, 344, 348*, 63
Cameron, A 59
Candidum . . . . . *line 602*, 69, 70
Cantabri 55
Capestang, Étang de 69

Carpenter, R . . v, 3n, 51, 52, 53,
  58, 60, 63, 64
Cartagena 63
Cartare . . . . . . line 255, 57, 59
Carthage . . . lines 114, 311, 376,
  54, 60, 61
Carthaginians . . . ix, 27n, 51, 53,
  55, 60, 61, 63, 69
Carthago Nova 62, 63
Caryanda . . . . . lines 42, 372, 50
Caspian Sea . . . . . lines 399, 403
Cassius 41n, 71
Cassius, mons . . . . . line 259, 57
Castellón de Ampurias 67
Castellón, Estangue de 67
Cástulo 59
Cecylistrium . . . . . . line 703, 73
Celebanticum . . . . . line 525, 66
Celts . . . . . . lines 133, 135, 53,
  54, 55, 65, 71
Cempsi . . . . . . lines 195, 200,
  257, 301, 55, 57
Cempsicum . . . . . . line 182, 55
Ceretes . . . . line 550, 68
Cerro de Asperillo 57
Cerro de San Cristóbal 59
Cesse 66
Cévennes 71
Champion vi
Chrysus . . . . . . line 419, 61, 62
Cilbicene . . . . line 422, 62
Cilbiceni . . . . . . lines 255, 303,
  57, 59
Cilbus . . . . line 320, 59, 60
Cilpe 59
Cimenice . . . . line 622, 71
Cinorus . . . . line 596, 70
Cirta 70
Clahilci . . . . line 675, 72
Clape . . . . ix, 69
Classius . . . . . line 621, 41n, 71

Cleon . . . . line 48, 50
Coimbra 55
Colason 71
Colazou 71
Coll Alba 66
Columns of Atlas 60
Coria 59
Costa da Gale 55
Couronne 73
Crabasiae . . . . line 489, 65
Crau, la 73
Crebère 67
Creus 67
Crimea 49
Cullera 65
Cynetes . . . . lines 201, 205, 223,
  55, 56
Cyneticum . . . lines 201, 566, 56
Cypsela . . . . . . line 527, 66, 67

Dala 72
Daliterni . . . . line 675, 72
Damastes . . . . . . lines 46, 372,
  5n, 25n, 50, 61
Damnastock 72
Darius 50
Demophilus 60
Denia 64, 65
Denmark 52, 53
Dertosa 65
Descriptio Orbis Terrae . . . lines
  72-3, 7n, 51, 61
Dianium 64
Diodorus 72
Dionysius Periegetes . . line 331,
  7n, 51, 61
dos Caes 56
Douarnenez 52
Draganes . . . . line 197, 55
Duero 55

Ebro . . . . *lines 248, 503*, 65
Egypt 57
Ελαιος 65
Elaisos 65
Elesyces . . . . *line 586*, 69
Elna 68
England 9n
Ensérune 68
Ephorus . . . . vi, 50, 61
Epicureans . . . *line 652*, 43n, 72
Erbi . . . . *line 244*, 57
Erebea . . . . *line 244*, 57
Ερεβος 57
Erythia . . . . . *lines 309, 314*, 60
Espartel 60
Espichel 55
Etmaneum gens . . . . *line 300*, 59
Etruscans 66
Euctemon . . . *lines 47, 337*, 350, 23n, 50, 60
Europa . . . . *lines 203, 333, 353, 375, 418, 694*
Euthymenes v

Feliu de Guixols, San 66
Ferraria 63
Figo, Mount 56
Fonollera 66
Frisians 53

Gades . . . . . . ix, 51, 58, 59, 60
Gadir . . . . . . *lines 85, 267, 269*, 51, 52
Gale, Costa da 55
Gallaeci 55
Garcia y Bellido, A 61, 62, 66, 68
Gata 62
Gaul(s) . . . . . . *line 638*, 64, 68, 69, 71, 72, 73
Geneva, Lake 72

Georgics 56
Geron . . . . . . *lines 263, 304*, 58
Gibraltar, Straits of 55, 61
Gisinger, F 50
Gletsch 72
Grosa 63
Gruissan 69
Guadiana 56
Guadiero 61
Gymnesia . . . . *line 467*, 64
Gymnetes . . . . *line 464*, 64

Haesican 41n
Hecataeus . . . . *line 42*, v, 50, 63
Heledus . . . . *line 592*, 69
Helice . . . . *line 590*, 69
Hellanicus . . . . *line 43*, 50
Helvetii 72
Hemeroscopium . . . *line 476*, 64
Hérault 70
Herbi . . . . *line 244*, 57
Hercules . . . . *lines 86, 115, 163, 326, 327, 341, 354, 358, 562, 51, 60, 73*
Herma . . . . *lines 323, 324, 329, 336, 444, 60, 62*
Herna . . . . *line 463*, 64
Herodotus . . . . . *line 49*, 50, 69
Hespericus aestus . . . *line 398*, 61
Hiberi . . . . *lines 250, 472, 480,*
(See also *Iberians*)   *552, 613,*
                             19n, 64
Hiberia . . . . *line 253*, 57
Hiberus . . . *lines 248, 503*, ix, 57
Hierne 52
Hierni . . . . *line 111*
Higuer 54
Himilco . . . *lines 117, 383, 412, 27n, 53*
Hind, J 68

Hi(v)eriyo 52
Holder . . . . vii, viii
Hudson vii
Huelva, Gulf of 51, 56, 62
Hylactes . . . . line 497, 65
Hyrcana unda . lines 399, 403, 65
Hystra . . . . line 497, 65

Iberians . . . . ix, 54, 57, 64, 65,
(See also Hiberi) 66, 68, 70
Ibiza 64
Ifach 63, 64
Ἰγλῆτες 59
Ileates . . . . line 302, 59
Ilercavones 64
Ilerda . . . . line 475, 64
Ilergetes 64
Ilicitanus sinus 63
Indicetes 66
Indicorum salum . . . . . . line 400
Indigetes . . . . lines 523, 532, 66
Ionians 43n, 50, 52, 72
Iovis mons 67
Ireland 9n, 52
Isla de la Paloma 61
Isla de Leon 60
Isla del Perejil 61
Italy 71

Jannoray, J 70, 73
Jávea 64
Joliette, La 73
Juba . . . . . line 280, vi, 21n, 59
Júcar 63, 64, 65, 70
Jullian 70
Jutland . . . . ix, 53

Lamboglia, N . . . 35n, 66, 67, 68
Latera . . . . line 559, 68
Lattes 68
Lebedontia . . . . line 509, 66
Lebedos 66
Leixâo 56
Lemannus Lacus 45n, 72
Lemenici . . . . line 676, 45n, 72
Lemenicus ager . . . . line 676, 72
Leon, Isla de 60
Lerida 64
Leucate, Étang de 69
Leuk 72
Libron 69
Libya . . lines 88, 329, 444, 694,
21n, 59
Libyphoenices . . line 421, 29n, 61
Ligurians . . . . . . lines 132, 135,
196, 613, 628, ix, 15n, 52,
53, 54, 55, 59, 68, 70, 72, 73
Ligustinus lacus . . . line 284, 59
Liron 69
Lisbon, Bay of 55
Livy 51
Loule 56
Lunae insula . . . line 367, 61, 62
Lusitanians 15n
Lycaon . . . . line 131, 53
Lydia 51, 59

Maccus 60
Maeoticum aequor . . . line 32, 49
Maguelonne 71
Malaca . . . lines 131, 426, 60, 61
Malacha . . . . line 426, 62
Málaga 62
Malestrou 73
Malodes . . . . line 535, 67
Manguio 71
Mansa . . . . line 616, 71
Mar Menor 63
Marismilla, La 58
Martín, G 64
Marx, Fr 49, 58
Massiena urbs . . . . . line 452, 63

Massieni . . . . *lines 422, 450,* 62
Massilia . . . . . . *lines 560, 704,*
    v, viii, ix, 41n, 71, 72, 73
Massiliotes . . 37n, 52, 53, 54, 70
Mastia 62, 63
Mastrabala . . . . *line 701,* viii, 73
Masua 71
Matthews, J 58
Maurenbrecker, B 50, 57
Mauretania 21n
Meca, Mount 60
Medas 67
Mediterranean . . . . . . v, viii, 61
Mela, Pomponius . . . 61, 63, 67,
    68, 71
Menace . . . . . *lines 427, 431,* 62
Menor, Mar 63
Mesua 71
Meuse 71
Méze 71
Minerva . . . . *line 495,* 65
Mistrel 71
Mongo 67
Montgo 66
Montgrí 66, 67
Montsía 65
Muga 68
Müllenhoff vii
Müller, C 45n
Mytilene 50

Naccararum palus . . *line 492,* 65
Namnatius portus . . . *line 449,* 63
Narbo 69
Naro . . . . *line 587,* 69
Nao, Cape 23n, 31n, 60,
    63, 64
Naustalo . . . . *line 616,* 71
Nearchi . . . . *line 700,* 73
Nevada, Sierra 62
Noctiluca . . . . . *line 429,* 61, 62

Northern Pillars 51, 52
Nuix, J M 66

Octavianus . . . . *line 279*
Oder 52
Oestrymnic Islands . . *line 130,* 53
Oestrymnici . . . . *line 155,*
    ix, 52, 53, 54
Oestrymnides . . *lines 96, 113,* 52
Oestrymnis . . . . . *lines 91, 154,*
    52, 53, 54
Oikonomides, Al N 67
Οἰστρύμνιοι 52
Old Port 73
Oleum . . . . *line 505,* 65
Onussa Cherronesi . . . . *line 491,*
    33n, 65
Ophiussa . . . . . . *lines 148, 152,*
    172, 196, 11n, 13n, 53, 54, 55
Ophiussae prominens . . *lines 171-*
    172, 56
Oranus . . . . *line 612,* 70
Orb 69
Orobus . . . . *line 592,* 69
Oropesa 65
Ortegal 54
Ortellius vii
Ossismi 52
Ὀστίωνες 52
Ouessant 51, 52
Onions 69
Ovid 53

Palaeopolis (Ampurias) 67
Pallas 70
Palmar 65
Paloma, Isla de la 61
Palos 63
Pausanias 57
Pausimachus . . . . . . *line 45,* 50
Peloponnesus 11n

Pelops . . . . *line 153*
Peñón de Peñíscola 65
Percebeira 55
Perejil, Isla del 61
Periplus . . . . . v, viii, ix, 50, 51,
    52, 53, 56, 57, 60, 61, 63,
    64, 66, 67, 68, 69, 71
Persicus fluctus . . . . . . *line 400*
Phileas . . . . *lines 43, 695*,
    5n, 45n, 50
Phocaeans 17n, 51, 55, 57,
    59, 60, 62, 64
Phoenicians 29n, 54, 55,
    58, 60, 61
Pillars of Hercules . *lines 86, 341*
(See also *Abila* and   355, viii,
  Calpe)   27n, 51, 61
Piplae . . . . *line 585*
Pisanus . . . . vii, 35n, 47n
Pithou viii
Pityussa . . . . . *line 470*, 29n, 62
Plaine de Fourques 72
Plana 63
Planasse 69
Plautus . . . . *line 347*, 60
Plaza de Pals 66
Pliny 29n, 63, 68
Poetanion . . . . *line 199*, 55
Pointe du Raz 52
Polybius 63
Polygium . . . . *line 615*, 70
Pomponius Mela 61, 63, 67,
    68, 71
Pontus . . . . *line 2*, 49
Port Vendres 68
Posidonius 72
Probus . . . . *lines 1, 24, 51, 632*,
    vi, 5n, 49
Provence vii
Ptolemy 57, 61, 63
Puerto de Selva de Mar . . 67, 68

Pyrene . . . . *lines 559, 562*,
    37n, 68, 72
Pyrenees . . . *lines 472, 492, 533,
    555, 565*, viii, 11n, 54,
    66, 67, 68
Pytheas . . . . v, 52

Rehm 60
Rhine 71
Rhode see Rosas
Rhone . . . . *lines 626, 631, 691*,
    31n, 41n, 50, 51,
    57, 64, 70, 71, 72
Rhony 70
Rhoscynus . . . . *line 567*, 68
Ripoll, E 66
Rius y Serra v
Roca 55, 56
Rome 61
Rosas 67, 68
Rosas, Gulf of 67
Rosellón 68

Sabinal 62
Sacer mons . . . . . . *line 504*, 65
Sacred Cape 55, 56
Sado 55
Sagres 56
Saguntum 65
Salado de Conil 60
Salauris . . . . *line 513*, 66
Sallust . . . . *line 33*, 50, 57
Salon 66
Saluvii 73
Salyes . . . . . *line 701*, viii, 73
Sancti Petri 61
Saint Blaise 73
Saint Martin 69
Saint Vincent, Cape 55, 60
Sainte Lucie 69
Samos . . . . *line 45*, 50

San Cristobal, Cerro de 59
San Feliu de Guixols 66
San Sebastian 60
Sanlacar 59
Santa Maria 56
Santa Maria de la Rabida 56
Saone 71
Sardum mare . . . . line 150
Sargasso Sea 53
Sarna . . . . line 497, 65
Saturnus . . . . . . lines 165, 216
Savory, H N 52, 55
scalae Hannibalis 67
Scandanavia 53
Schrader 15n
Schulten, A . . . . . v, vi, vii, viii,
   ix, 7n, 9n, 11n, 15n, 35n, 41n,
   49, 50, 51, 52, 54, 55, 56, 57,
   58, 59, 60, 61, 62, 63, 64, 65,
            66, 67, 68, 71
Scotland 52, 53
Scylax . . . . lines 44, 372, 50, 61
Scythia 53
Seeck, O 49
Sefes . . . . lines 195, 199, 54, 55
Segura 63
Selbyssina 62
Sellus . . . . line 507, 66
Selva del Mar 67, 68
Sertorius 57
Sete 70
Setius . . . lines 608, 609, 629, 70
Setubal 55
Seville 58
Sexi 60, 61
Sicana . . . . line 479, 65
Sicanus . . . . line 469, 64
Sierra de Balaguer 65
Sierra Nevada 62
Sige . . . . line 46, 50
Sigean 69

Sigeuni 50
Silleiro 54
Siturus . . . . line 433, 62
Sitges 66
Situs Ponti . . . . line 2, 50
Sordices . . . . line 570
Sordus amnis . . . . . line 574, 69
Sordus populus . . . . . lines 552,
                      554, 68
Soulier 69
Spain . . . . . viii, ix, 7n, 9n, 11n,
   51, 52, 54, 55, 59, 64, 66, 71
Stichtenoth, D 52
Strabo 52, 55, 59, 72
Straits of Gibraltar 55, 61
Strongyle . . . . line 453, 63
Sun, Column of . . . . . . line 646
Sweden 52
Syrtes 29n

Tabarca 63
Tader 63
Tajo 55
Tarascon 72
Tarraco . . . . line 519
Tarragona 66
Tarshish 51, 58
Tartarus 17n, 57
Tartessians . . . . . lines 113, 179,
   223, 254, 309, 332, 423,
   428, 463, v, ix, 52, 57,
            59, 62, 63, 64
Tartessus . . . . lines 85, 269,
   v, 13n, 19n, 23n, 50,
   51, 57, 58, 60, 64, 68
Tartessus River . . . . . lines 225,
            284, 57, 58, 59, 71
Tauricus pontus . . . . . line 2, 49
Taurus . . . . . . lines 610-11, 70
Tavira 56
Tecum 68

Telis 68
Temenicum 45n
Tenebrium 63
Ter 66
Terifa 61
Teffaco 66
Tertis 51
Tertosa 65
Tet 68
Tetis 68
Tetum 68
Thau, Étang de 70
Theline .... *line 690*, 72
Theodorus .... *line 456*, 63
Thucydides .... *line 50*, 50
Thyrius ..... *line 595*, 39n, 70
Timaeus 72
Tinto 57
Tolon, Étang de 67
Toni stagnum ..... *line 544*, 67
Tononita rupes .... *line 545*, 68
Torre del Mar 62
Torroella de Moutgri 67
Tossa, Cape de 66
Trafalgar, Cape 60
Tres Forcas 62
Trete .... *line 452*, 63
Tristia 53
Tulingi 72
Turia 65
Turicus 70
Tursa 51
Tylangii ..... *line 674*, 45n, 72
Tyrichae .... *line 498*, 65
Tyris .... *line 482*, 65
Tyrius .... *line 482*, 65

Ullastret 66
Unger 39n

Valencia 65

Vascones .... *line 251*, 57
Velez 62
Veneris insula .... *line 315*
Veneris iugum ... *lines 158, 437, 443*, 54, 62
Vergil 56
Vic 71
Vicus .... *line 616*, 71
Villaronga, L 66
Vinalapo 64
Vistre 70

Warmington vi
Wernsdorf vii
West Reef 63

Zephyris, arx . *lines 227, 238*, 56
Zephyris, ora .... *line 564*
Zephyrus ..... *lines 225-26*, 56

APPENDIX

The Editio Princeps of Avienus' *Ora Maritima*

The text of Avienus' *Ora Maritima* depends upon one single source, the *editio princeps* published at Venice in 1488.* The manuscript that Abraham Ortellius collated has itself been lost and we have only a few readings, which are preserved in the Leiden MS XXI. Schulten considers the manuscript of Ortellius to be worthless since it merely copies the printed version of 1488. The variants are Ortellius' conjectures. A second manuscript, Codex Ambrosianus D.52, contains lines 52 to 163 of the *Ora Maritima*, but offers no significant variants, and it too may be a copy of the printed version. Thus we are left with one source for the vast part of the text, namely, *the editio princeps*.

The *editio princeps* had as its editor and publisher, Victor Pisanus. In his introductory letter, Pisanus, however, gives credit to Georgia Valla for inspiring him in a recent conversation to publish learned writings on astronomy ("astrology" is the actual word he used) and medicine. The title page also gives credit to one Antonio de Strada, who was perhaps a generous patron who made the publication possible.

The editio princeps is a quarto sized book of 119 pages, 57 of which contain works by Avienus (dedicatory poem, a translation of Aratus' *Phaenomena*, the *Descriptio Orbis Terrae*, and the *Ora Maritima*). Following his intention of printing learned writings in astronomy, Pisanus included fragments of Germanicus' translation of Aratus' *Phaenomena* together with a commentary on those verses. There followed fragments of Cicero's translation of that same astronomical work. Finally, Pisanus published Serenus' work in medicine.

The critical apparatus of Schulten's text is rather thorough and very exact. Thus most emendations of the *editio princeps* are noted, but not every variant is indicated. Thus in this edition of Avienus' *Ora Maritima*, I include a facsimile of the 1488 Venice text. The student may examine the original text and weigh scholars' textual conjectures. Some of the gross errors in the text are merely printing mistakes, but surely the text is often corrupt and needs scholarly emendation. Barring the unlikely discovery of a manuscript, we are left with the *editio princeps* as our sole authority for the text of the *Ora Maritima*. Hence I include it in this edition.

---

*The books is even more precisely dated to *VIII Kal Nov.*, October 25th, 1488.

Semper in expertes famæ per inhofpita degunt
Arua procul nullis funt digne deniq̃ mufis
At tu phœbe pater nos clari turba camœnæ
Nominis aonio famam infpirate labori
RVFI FESTI DESCRIPTIO ORBIS TERRAE EXPLI
CIT.   INCIPIT ORAE MARITIMAE LIBER PRI
MVS FELIX.
        Væfiffe temet fæpe cogitans probe
        Animo atq̃ fenfu taurici ponti finus
q   Capi ut ualeret his probabili fide
        Quos diftenerent fpatia terrarum extima
        Subi libenter id laboris ut tibi
Defideratum carmine hoc clarefceret
Fas non putaui quippe prolixa die
Non fubiacere fenfui formam tuo
Regionis eius quam uetuftis paginis
Et qua per omnem fpūs noftri diem
Secretiore lectione acceperam
Alii inuidere nanq̃ quod difpendio
Tibi haud fit ullo oreftis & durreor
His addo & illud liberum temet locum
Mihi effet amor fanguinifq̃ uinculo
Neq̃ fat fit iftud mi cete litteras
Hiantibus que faucibus ueftarum abdita
Haufiffe femper effe patuli pectoris
Senfu capacem talium iugem fitim
Tuo effe cordi & effe te præ cæteris
Memorem intimati cur inefficaciter
Secreta rerum in non tenacem effūderem
In non fequacē quis profunda ogganniat
Multa ergo multa compulere me probe
Efflagitatam rem tibi ut per foluerem
Quin & parent credidi officium fore
Defidaratum fi tibi locupleclus
Profufiufq̃ mufa promeret mea
Dare expetitum quippe non pare uiri eft
Augere porrho muneris fumma noui
Mentis benigne fatq̃ liberalis eft

Editio princeps: lines 1-31

Interrogasti si tenes mæotici
Situs qui esset æquoris Sallustium
Noram id dedisse dicta & eius omnibus
Præiudicatæ autoritatis ducier
Non abnuebam ad eius igitur inclytam
Descriptionem qua locorum formulam
Imaginemque expressor efficax stili
Et ueritatis pene in optutus dedit
Leporem linguæ multa rerum uiximus
Ex plurimorum supta comentariis
Hæc ad eus istic quippe erit mille suis
Hellanicus que lesbius phileus quoque
Atheniensis cariæ ditus scylax
Pausimachus ille prisca qué genuit samos
Quin & damastus nobili natus signe
Rhodonque bacoris ortus euctemon quoque
Populari urbis atticæ siculus cleon
Herodotus ipse thyriustum qui decus
Magnum loquendi est atticus thucydides
Hic porrho hebis pars mei cordis probe
Quicquid per æquor insularum attollitur
Per æquor illud scilicet quod post caua
Hiatis orbis a freto tartesio
Atlanticisque fluctibus procul sictam
Inusque glæbam proruit nrm mare
Sinus curuos atque prominentia
Vt se supino porrigat littus situ
Vt longe in undas inferant sese iuga
Celsæque ut urbes alluantur æquore
Quis ortus amnis maximo effuderit
Vt prona ponti gurgitem intrent flumina
Vt ipsæ rursum sæpe cingant insulas
Sinuentque late ut tute portus brachia
Vt explicentur stagna ceu iaceant lacus
Scruposum ut alti uerticem montes leuent
Stringatque nemora ut unda cani gurgitis
Laboris autem terminus nostri hic erit
Scythicum ut profundum & æquor euxini sali

Editio princeps: 32-69

Et si quae in illo marmore insulae tument
Edisserantur reliqua porro scripta sunt
Nobis in illo plenius uolumine
Quod de orbis oris partibusq; fecimus
Vt aperta uero tibimet intimatio
Sudoris huius & laboris sit mei
Narratione opusculi paulo altius
Exordiemur tu ex intimum iecur
Prolata conde nanq; fulcit haec fides
Petita longe & eruta ex autoribus
Terrae patentis orbis effusae iacent
Orbiq; rursus unda circúfunditur
Sed qua profundum se met insinuat salum
Oceano abusq; ut gurges hic nostri maris
Longe explicetur est atlanticus sinus
Hic gadir urbs est dicta tartessus prius
Hic sunt columnae pertinacis herculis
Abila atq; calpae leua dicti caespitis
Libye propinque stalia duro perstrepunt
Septrentione sed loco certae tenent
Et prominentis hic iugi surgit caput
Oestrymnin istud dixit aeuum antiquius
Molesq; celsa saxei fastigii
Tota in tepentem maxime uergit notum
Sub huius autem prominentis uertice
Sinus dehiscit incolis oestrymninus
In quo insulae sese exerunt oestrymnides
Laxe iacentes & metallo diuites
Stanni atq; plumbi multa uis hic gentis est
Superbus animus efficax solertia
Negociandi cura iugis omnibus
Notusq; cum bis turbidum late fretum
Er beluosi gurgitem oceani secant
Non hi carinas quippe pinu texere
Facere morem non abiete ut usus est
Curuant fasello sed rei admiraculum
Nauigia iunctis semper aptant pellibus
Corioq; uastum saepe percurrunt salum

Editio princeps: 70-107

Ast hinc duobus in sacram sic insulam
Dixere priscis solibus cursus rati est
Haec inter undas multam caespitem iacet
Eamque late gens hiernorum colit
Propinqua rursus insula albionum patet
Tartesusque inter minos oestrumnidum
Negociandi mos erat carthaginis
Et iam colonis & uulgus inter herculis
Agitans colunas haec adhibant aequora
Quae himilcopaenus mensibus uix quattuor
Vt ipse semet rem probasse retulit
Enauigantem posse transmitti adserit
Sic nulla late flabra propellunt ratem
Sic regnis humor aequoris pigri stupet
Adiicient illud plurimum inter gurgites
Extare fucum & saepe uirgulti uice
Retinere pupim dicit hic nihilominus
Non in profundum terga dimitti maris
Paruoque quarum uix supertexi solum
Obire semper huc & hunc pontiferas
Nauigia lenta & languide repentia
Inter natare beluas si quis dehinc
Ab insulis oestrymnicis lembum audeat
Vrgere in undas axe qua lycaonis
Rigescit aethra caespitem ligurgum subit
Cassum incolarum nanque celtarum manu
Crebrisque dudum praeliis uacuata sunt
Liguresque pulsi ut saepe fors aliquos agit
Venere in ista quae perhorrentis tenent
Plerunque dumos creber his scrupus locis
Rigidaeque rupes atque montium minae
Coelo inferuntur & fugax gens haec quidem
Diu inter arta cautium duxit diem
Secreta ab undis nam sali metuens erat
Priscum ob periculum post quies & otium
Securitate roborante audaciam
Persuasit altis deuehi cubilibus
Atque in marinos iam locos descendere

Editio princeps: 108-145

Post illa rursum quae super facti sumus
Magnus patescit aequoris suffinus
Ophiusa madus que rursum ab huius littore
Internum ad aequor qua mare insinuare se
Dixi ante terris quodq3 sardum nuncupant
Septem dierum tenditur reditu uiae
Ophiussa porro tanta panditur latus
Quantam iacere pelopis audis insulam
Graiorum in agro haec dicta primo oestrymnis
Locus & arua oestrymnicis habitantibus
Post multa serpens effugauit incolas
Vacuáq3 glaebam nominis fecit sui
Procedit inde in gurgitis ueneris iugum
Circulatratq3 pontus in sucas duas
Tenue ob locorum inhospita saryium
Rursum tumescit promineas in asperum
Septentrionum cursus aut hinc classibus
Vsq3 in colunas efficacis herculis
Quinq3 est dierum post pelagia est insula
Herbarum abundans ad saturno sacra
Sed uis in illa tanta naturalis est
Vt siquis hanc in'nauigando accesserit
Mox excitetur propter insulam mare
Quatiatur ipsa & omne subsiliat solum
Alte intremescens caetero adsteni uicem
Pelago silente prominens surgit dehinc
Ophiussae moras abq3 arui iugo
In haec locorum bidui cursus patet
At qui dehiscit inde prolixe sinus
Non totus uni facile uauigabilis
Vento recedit nunquam medium aceris
Zephyro uehente reliqua deposcunt notum
Et rusus inde si petat quisquam pede
Tartessiorum litus exuperet uiam
Vix luce quarta siquis ad nostrum mare
Malaceq3 portum semitam tetenderit
In'quinq3 soles est iter tum cepresicum
Iugum intumescit subiacet porro insula

Edition princeps: 146-183

Achale uocata ab incolis agresti fides
Narrationis præ rei miraculo
Sed quam frequens auctoritas sal fulciat
Aiunt in huius insule confiniis
Nunquam esse formam gurgiti reliquo parem
Splendore ubiq; quippe inesse fluctibus
Vitri ad nitorem & per profundam marmoris
Coeaneam in undis esse certum imaginem est
Confodiat illic æquor imunda luto
Memorant uetusti semper atq; sordibus
Vt feculentos gurgites herescere
Cépsi atq; sæfes arduos collis habent
Ophiusse in agro propter hos pernix lucis
Draganúq; proles sub niuosa maxime
Septentrione conlocauerant larem
Poetanion autem est insula ad se fumum latet
Patulusq; portus inde cépsis adiacent
Populi cynetum tyneticum iugum
Qua syderalis lucis inclinatio est
Alte cum escens ditis europe extimum
Imbeluosi uergit oceani si salum
Ana animis illic per cynetas effluit
Sulcatq; glæbam panditur rursus sinus
Cauusq; cæspes in meridiem patet
Memorato aliamin gemina sese flumina
Scindunt repente per que prædicti sinus
Crassum liquorem quippe pinguesci luto
Omne hic profundum lenta trudunt agmina
Hic insularum se met alte subrigit
Vertex duarum nominis minor indiga est
Aliam uocauit mox tenax agonida
Inhorret inde rupibus cautes sacra
Saturni & ipsa feruet inlisum mare
Littusq; latus saxeum distenditur
Hirtæ hic capellæ & multus incolis caper
Dumosa semper intererrant cæspitum
Castrorum in usu sumet nauticis uelamina
Productio restet graues setas alunt

Editio princeps: 184-221

Hinc dictum adáne solis unius uia est
Genti & cynetum hic terminus tartesus
Ager his adheret adluitq̃ cæspitem
Tartesus amnis inde tenditur iugum
Zephyro sacratum deniq̃ arcis sumitas
Zephyris uocata celsa sed ad fastigia
Iugo eriguntur uertici multus timor
Conscendit auras & super syderis q̃si
Caligo semper nubilum condit caput
Regio omnis inde maxime herboso solo est
Nebulosa iuge his incolis conuexa sunt
Coactus aer atq̃ crassior dies
Noctisq̃ more ros frequens nulla ut solea
Flabra inferuntur nullus æthram discutit
Superne uenti spiritus pigra incumbat
Caligo terras & solum late madet
Zephyridos arcem siquis excedat rate
Et inferatur gurgiti nri maris
Flabris uehetur protinus fauoni
Iugum inde rursus & sacrum infernæ deæ
Diuesq̃ fanum penetral abstrusi caui
Aditumq̃ cæcum multa propter est palus
Et rephaea dicta quin & herbi ciuitas
Stetisse fertur his locis prisca die
Quæ preliorum absumpta pestatibus
Famam atq̃ nomen sola liquit cæspiti
Anhyberus inde manat amnis & locos
Fecundat unda plurimi & ipso ferunt
Dictos hyberos non ab illo flumine
Quod inquieto suo uascomas prælabitur
Nam quicquid amnem gentis huius adiacet
Occiduum ad axem hiberiam cognominant
Pars porro eoa continet tartesios
Et cilbicenos cartare post insula est
Eamq̃ pridem influxe satis est fides
Tenuere cempsi proximorum postea
Pulsi duello uaria qua est tum loca
Se protulere cassius inde mons tumet

Editio princeps: 222-259

Et graia ab ipso lingua caſſiterum prius
Stannum uocauit inde fani eſt prominens
Et quæ uetuſtum græcie nomen tenet
Gerontis ars eſt eminus nanq3 ex ea
Geryona quondam nuncupatum acepimus
Hic ora late ſunt ſinus tarteſii
Dictoq3 ab uni in hæc locorum puppibus
Via eſtdiei gadir hic eſt oppidum
Nam punicorum lingua conſeptum locum
Gadir uocabat ipſa tarteſſus prius
Cognomina eſt multa & opulens ciuitas
Aeuo uetuſto nunc egena nunc breuis
Nunc deſtituta nunc ruinarum ager eſt
Nos hoc locorum præter herculanea
Solemnitatem uidimus miri nihil
Atuis in illis tanta uel tamen decus
Aetate priſca ſub fide rerum fuit
Rex ut ſuperbus omniumq3 præpotens
Quos gens habebat forte tum maurusia
Octauiano principi acceptiſſimus
Et literarum ſemper in ſtudio iuba
Interfluoq3 ſeparatus æquore
Inluſtriore ſemet urbis iſtius
Duum iuratu crederet ſed inſulam
Tarteſſus amnis ex liguſtino lacu
Per aperta fuſus undiq3 ab lapſu ligat
Neq iſte tractu ſimplici prouoluitur
Vnuſue ſulcat ſubiacentem cæſpitem
Tria ora quippe parte eoi luminis
Infert in agros ore biſgemino quoq3
Meridiana ciuitatis adluit
At mons paludem incubit argentarius
Sic a uetuſtis dictus ex ſpc̄ ſui
Stagno iſte nanq3 latera plurimo nitet
Magisq3 in auras eminus lucem euomit¿
Cum ſol ab igni celſa perculerit iuga
Idem amnis aut fluctibus ſtagni grauis
Ramenta uolut inuehitq3 mœnibus

Editio princeps: 260-297

Diues metallum qua dehinc ab æquore
Salsi fluenti uasta per medium soli
Regio redit gens & maneum accolit
Atq̃ inde rursus usq̃ cempsorum sata
Ileates agros efferaci porrigunt
Maritima uero cibiceni possident
Gerontis arcem & prominés fani ut supra
Sumus elocuti distinet medium salum
Interq̃ celsa cautium cedit sinus
Iugum ad secundum flumen amplum euoluit
Tartesiorum mons dehinc attollitur
Siluis opacus hinc erythia est insula
Diffusa glebam & uiris olim punici
Habuere primo quippe eam cartaginis
Prisce coloni interfluoq̃ scinditur
At continentem quinq̃ per stadia modo
Erythia ab arce qua diei occasus est
Veneri marinæ consecrata est insula
Templúq̃ in illa ueneris & poene sal cauum
Oraculumq̃ monte ab illo quem tibi
Horrere siluis dixeram inueneris
Litus redine & molle harenarum iacet
In quas besilus atq̃ cilbus flumina
Vergent fluentum post in occiduum diem
Sacrum superbas erigit cautes iugum
Locum hunc uocauit herma quondam græcia
Est herma porrho cæspitum munitio
Interfluúq̃ altrinsecus munit locus
Aliiq̃ rursus herculis dicuntur ani uiam
Strauisse quippe maria fertur hercules
Iter ut pateret facile captiuo gregi
Porrho illud herma iure sublibyq̃ soli
Fuisse pridem plurimi auctores ferunt
Nec respuendus testis est dionysius
Libye esse finem qui docet tartessium
Europe in agro quod uocari ab incolis
Sacrum indicaui prominens subducitur
Locus utrosq̃ interfluit tenue fretum

Editio princeps: 298-335

Quod herma porrho aut herculis dictum est uia
Amphipolis urbis incola hoc demon ait
Non plus here longitudinis modo
Quam porriguntur centum & octo milia
Et distineri   milibus tribus
Hic herculanæ stant colūnæ quas modum
Vtriusq̃ haberi continentis legimus
Sunt parua porrho saxa prominentia
Ab illa atq̃ calpe calpe hispano solo
Maurisiorum est ab illa nanq̃ ab illa uocant
Gens punicorum mons quod altus barbaro est
Idest latino dicti ut autor plautus est
Calpeq̃ rursum in græcia spes caua
Teretesq̃ uisu nūcupatur & iugi
Atheniensis dicit eucte monitem
Non esse saxa aut uertices adsurgere
Parte ex utraq̃ cæspitem libyci soli
Europæ & oram memorat insulas duas
Iter acerui nūcupari has herculis
Ait colūnas est adia tritiginta refert
Has distinere horrere siluis undiq̃
Inhospitata sq̃ semper esse nauticis
Inesse quippe dicit ollis herculis
Et templa & haras inuehi aduenas rates
Deo litare abire festino pede
Nefas putatum demorati in insulis
Circum atq̃ iuxta plurimo
Manere tradit tenue prolixe mare
Nauigia honusta adire non ualent locos
Breue ob fluentum & pingue littori lutum
Sed si uoluntas forte quem subegerit
Adire fanum propter ad lunæ insulam
Agere carinam eximere classi pondera
Leuiq̃ cymba uix superferri salo
Sed ad colūnas quicquid interfunditur
Vnde æstuantis studia septem uix ait
Damascus esse cariæ dictus scylax
Medium fluentum inter columnas adserit

Editio princeps: 336-373

Tantum patete q̄tus æstus bosporo est
Vltra has colūnas pp europæ latet
Vicos & urbis incolæ carthaginis
Tenuere quōdam mos at ollis hic erat
Vt planior texerent fundo rates
Quo cymba tergum fusior breuius mare
Prælaberetur porro in occiduam plaga
Ab his colunnis gurgitē esse in terminum
Late patere pelagus extendi salum
Himilco tradit nullus hæc adijt freta
Nullus carinas æquor illud intulit
Desint quod alto flabra propellentia
Nullusq̃ puppim spiritus cœli uiuet
Dehinc quod æthram quod amictu uestiat
Caligo se per nebula condat gurgitem
Et crassiorem nubilum perstet die
Oceanus iste est orbis effusi procul
Circum latratur iste pontus maximus
Hic gurges oras ambigens hic intimi
Salis inrigator hic parens nostri maris
Plerosq̃ quippe extrinsecus turbat sinus
Nostrumq̃ in orbem uis profundi inlabitur
Sed nos loquemur maximo tibi quttuor
Prima huius ergo in cæspitem insinuatio est
Hæsperius æstus atq̃ atlanticum salum
Hircana rursus unda caspium mare
Solo indicorum terga fluctum persici
Arabsq̃ gurges sub tepente iam noto
Hunc usus olim dixit oceanum uetus
Alterq̃ dixit mos atlanticum mare
Longo explicatur gurges huius ambitu
Produciturq̃ latere prolixe uago
Plerūq̃ porro tenue tenditur salum
Vt uix harenas sub iacenti occulat
Exuperat autem gurgitem fusus frequens
Atq̃ impeditur æstus hic uligine
Vis uel uarium pelagus omne internatat
Multusq̃ terror ex feris habitat freta

Editio princeps: 374-411

Hec olim hemelco pœnus oceano super
Spectasse semet & probasse retulit
Hæc nos ab imis punicorum analibus
Prolata longo tempore edidimus tibi
Nunc iam recursus ad priora sit stilo
Igitur colūnæ ut dixera libystidis
Europæ in agro aduersa surgit altera
Hic chrysus amnis intrat altum gurgitem
Vltra citraq̃ quattuor gentes colunt
Nam sunt feroces hoc loci liby phœnices
Sunt massieni regna selbyssina sunt
Feracis agri & diuitis tartesii
Qui porrigitur in calacticum sinum
Hos propter aūt mox iugum barbetium est
Malachæq̃ flumen urbe cum cognomine
Mæneace prior   uocata est sæculo
Tartesiorum uiris illic insula
Antistar urbem nectilucæ ab incolis
Sacrata pridem in insula stagnum quoq̃
Totusq̃ porrus oppidum minace super
Qua sese ab undis regio dicta subtrahit
Silurus alto mons tumet cacumine
Adsurgit inde uasta cautes & mare
Intrat profundam pinus hanc quondam frequens
Ex se uocari sub sono graio dedit
Phanumq̃ adusq̃ ueneris ac ueneris iugum
Littus recumbit porro in isto littore
Stetere crebre ciuitates antea
Phœnixq̃ multus habuit hos pridem locos
In hospitales nunc harenas porrigit
Deserat tellus orba cultorum sola
Squalent iacentq̃ ueneris abdito iugo
Spectatur herma cæspitis libyci procul
Quod ante dixi littus hic rursum patet
Vacuum incolarum nunc & abiecti soli
Porro ante & urbes hic stetere plurimæ
Populiq̃ multi concelebrant locos
Nam natius inde portus   op   se

Editio princeps: 412-449

Semassienum curuat alto ab æquore
Sinuqʒ in imo surgit altis mœnibus
Vrbs massiena post iugum traete eminet
Breuisqʒ iuxta strongile stat insula
Dehinc in huius insulæ confiniis
Immensa tergum latera diffundit palus
Theodorus illic nec stupori sit tibi
Quod in feroci barbaroqʒ stat loco
Cognomen huius græciæ accipis sono
Prorepit amnis ista phœnices prius
Loca incolebant rursus hinc se littoris
Fundunt harenæ & littus hoc tris insulæ
Cinxere late hic terminus quondam stetit
Tartesiorum hic herna ciuitas fuit
Gymnetes istos gens locos infederant
Nunc destitutus & dui incolis carens
Sibi sonorus alebus amnis effluit
Post hæc per undas insula est gymnesia
Populo incolarum quæ uetus nomen dedit
Adusqʒ cani prefluentis alueum
Pytuisse & inde proferunt sese insulæ
Baliaricarum late insularum dorsa sunt
Et contra hiberi inusqʒ pyrene iugum
Ius protollere propter interius mare
Late locuti prima eorum ciuitas
Ilerda surgit littus extendit dehinc
Steriles harenas hemerosco pium quoqʒ
Habita pridem hic ciuitas nunc iam solum
Vacuum incolarum languido stagno madet
Attollit inde se sitana ciuitas
Propinquo ab amni sic uocata hibericis
Neqʒ longe ad huius fluminis diuortio
Præstringit amnis tyrius oppidum tyrin
Ad qua recedit ab solo tellus procul
Dumosa late terga regio porrigit
Berybraces illic gens agrestis & ferox
Pecorum frequentis intererrabat greges
Hic lacte semet atqʒ pingui caseo.

Editio princeps: 450-487

Prædurea lentes proferebant spūm
Vicem ad ferarum post crabrasiæ iugum
Procedit alte ac nuda littorum iacent
Ad usqȝ cassæ herronesi terminos
Palus per illa naccararum extenditur
Hoc nomen isti nam pal   osdedit
Stagniqȝ medio parua surgit insula
Ferax oliui & hinc minerue sat sacra
Fuere pp ciuitates plurimæ
Quippe hic hylactes hystra sarna & nobilis
Tyrichæ stetere nomen oppido uetus
Gaiæ incolarum maxime memorabiles
Pre orbis oras nanqȝ præter cæspitis
Fecunditatem qua pecus qua palmitem
Qua dona flauæ cereris educat solum
Peregrina hibero subeuntur flumine
Iuxta superbum mons acer caput exerit
Oleumqȝ flumem proxuma agrorum secans
Geminos iugorum uertices interfluit
Mox quippe sellus nomen hoc monti est uetus
Adusqȝ celsa nubium subducitur
Ad stabatistum ciuitas lebedontia
Priore ædo nunc agerua cuius lare
Lustra & ferarum sustinet cubilia
Post hæc harenæ plurimo tracta iacent
Per quas sal auri oppidum quondam stetit
In quis et olim prisca callipolis fuit
Callipolis ill   menium
Proceritatem & celsam per fastigia
Subibat auras quæ laris uasti ambitu
Latere ex utroqȝ piscium semper ferax
Stagnum imprimebat inde carraco oppidum
Et barcilonum amœnas sedes ditium
Nam pandit illic tuta portus brachia
Vuetqȝ semper dulcibus tellus aquis
Post indigetes asperi se proferunt
Gens ista dura gens ferox uenatibus
Lustrisqȝ inherens tum iugum celebandicum

Editio princeps: 488-525

Inusq̃ salsam dorsa porrigit thetim
Hic adstitisse ciuitatem cypselam
Iam fama tantum est nulla nam uestigia
Prioris urbis asperum seruat solum
Dehiscit illic maximo portus sinu
Cauumq̃ late cespitem inrepit salum
Post que recumbit littus indiceticum
Pyrene adusq̃ prominentis uerticem
Post littus illud quod iacere diximus
Tractu supino se malo des exerit
Mons inter undas   tument sco
Geminusq̃ uer
Hos inter aut portus effuse iacet
Nullisq̃ flabris æquor est obnoxium
Sic omne late prælocatis rupibus
Latus ambiere cautium cacumina
Interq̃ saxa immobilis gurges latet
Quiescit æquor pelagus inclusum stupet
Stagnum inde toni montium in radicibus
Tononitæ que attollitur rumpis iugum
Per quæ sonorus uoluit æquor spumeum
Anystus amni & salum fluctu secat
Hæc propter undas atq̃ salsa sunt freta
At quicquid agri cedit alto a gurgite,
Cæretes omne & aucoceretes prius
Habuere duri nunc pari sub nomine
Gens est hiberum cor dus inde deniq̃
Populus agebat inter auios locos
Ac pertinentes usq̃ ad interius mare
Qua pini fertæ stant pyrenæ uertices
Inter ferarum lustra duceba
Et arua late & gurgitem ponti premit
Insordiceni cæspitis confinio
Quondam pyrenæ latera ciuitas diti flaris
Stetisse fertur hic que masiliæ incolæ
Negociorum sæpe uersabant uices
Sed in pyrenen ab colunnis herculis
Atlanticoq̃ gurgite & confinio

Editio princeps: 526-563

Zephyris oræ curfus eft celeri rati
Septem dierum poft pyrenæum iugum
Iacent harenæ littoris cynetici
Eafq late fulcat amnis rofchinus
Hoc fordicenæ ut diximus glæbe folum eft
Stagnum hic palus quæ quippe diffufæ patet
Et incolæ iftam fordicen cognominant
Præterq uafti gurgitis crepulas aquas
Nam propter amplum marginis laxe ambitum
Ventis tumefcit fæpe cellentibus
Stagno hoc ab ipfo fordus amnis effluit
Ru   effluentis hoftiis

Sinuatur alto & propria per difpendia
Cæfpes cauatur eripit unda longior
Molefq multa gurgitis diftenditur
Tris nanq in illo maximæ ftant infulæ
Saxifq duris pelagus interfunditur
Nec longe ab ifto cæfpitis rupti finus
Alter dehifcit infulafq quttuor
At prifcus ufus dixit has omnis piplas
Ambit profundo gens elefycum prius
Loca hæc tenebat atq naro ciuitas
Era ferocis maximum regni caput
Hic falfum in æquor amnis attagus ruit
Heliceq rurfus hic palus iufta dehinc
Befaram ftetiffe fama caffa tradidit
At nunc heledus nunc & orobus flumina
Vacuos per agros & ruinarum aggeres
Amœnitatis indices prifcæ meant
Nec longe ab iftis thyrius alto euoluitur
       Cinorus agmen

Num qua excitent fluctuum uolumina
Stematq femper gurgitem alcyonæ quies
Vertex ad huius cautis e regione fe

Editio princeps: 564-601

Illi eminenti porrigit quod candidum
Dixi uocari blasco propter insula est
Teretiqʒ forma cæspes editur salo
Incontinenti & inter adsurgentium
Capita iugorum rursum harenosi soli
Terga explicatur seqʒ fudunt littora
Orba incolarum setyus inde mons tumet
Procerus arcem & pinifer fecyi iugum
Radice fusa inusqʒ taurum pertinet
Taurum paludem nanqʒ gentici uocant
Orani propinquam fiumini huius alueo
Hibera tellus adqʒ ligies asperi
Inter secantur hic sat angusti laris
Tenuisqʒ censu ciuitas polygium est
Tum mansa uicus oppidúqʒ naustalo
Et urbs   hæsice gen sale

Eiusqʒ in æquor classius amnis influit
At cimenice regio discendit procul
Salso adfluento fusa multo cæspite
Et a prisca siluis nominis porrho auctor
Mons dorsa celsus huius imos aggeres
Stringit fluendo rhodanus atqʒ scrupeam
Molle imminentis intererrat æquore
Ligures ad undam semet interni maris
Secyena ab arce & rupe saxosi iugi
Procul extulere sed quasi exposcit locus
Rhodani in fluentum plenius tibi disseram
Stili imorantis pater tractatu improbe
Quippe amnis ortum gurgitis lapsum uagi
Quis iste gentis lambat undas fluminis
Quantoqʒ manet incolis compendio
Ft hostiorum fabimur diuortia
Niuosum in auras erigunt alpes iugū
A solis ortu & arua gallici sali
Intersecantur scrupeo fastigio

Editio princeps: 602-639

Et anhela semper flabra tempestatibus
Effusus ille & ore semet exigens
Hiantis antriui truci sulcat sola
Aquarum in ortu & fronte primo nauiger
Ad rupis illud erigentis se latus
Quod deditamne gentici cognominat
Solis colūnâ tanto enim fastígio
In usq celsa nubium subducitur
Merianus sol ut positu iugi
Conspicuus haud sit cum relaturus diem
Septentrionum acer serit confinia
Scis nam fuisse eiusmodi sententiam
Epicureorum non occasu premi
Nullo subire gurgites nunquam oculi
Sed obire mundum obliqua coeli currere
Animare terras alere lucis pabulo
Conuexa cúcta & inuicem regionibus
Cer   negari candidam phoebi facem
Resi

Meridianum cum secuerit orbitam
Cum lumen axi atlantico inclinauerit
Vt in supremos ignem hyperboreos agat
Ac hemonioco qua semet ortui ferat
Discreta in æthræ flectitur curuo ambitu
Metamq transit cunq nostro obtutui
Iubar negari terra nox coelo ruit
Cæceq nostra protinus tenebræ tegunt
Dies attillos clara tunc inluminat
Septentrionis qui superposito rigent
Cum rursus umbra noctis arctoos habet
Genus omne nostrum splendidum ducit diem
Meat amnis aut fonte per tylagios
Per daliternos per clahilcorum fata
Temenicum & agrum durasat uocabula
Auremq primam cuncta uulnerantia

Editio princeps: 640-677

Sed non silenda tibi met ob studium tuum
Nostramq̃ cura panditur porrho in decem
Vexis recursu gurgitū stagnum graue
Pleriq̃ tradunt inserit semet dehinc
Vasta in paludem quá uetus mos græciæ
Vocitauit accion quæ præcipites aquas
Stagni per æquore gerit rursum effluus
Arctans qua sese fluminum ae forma dehinc
Atlanticos in gurgites nostrum in mare
Et occidentem contuens euoluitur
Patulasq̃ harenas quinq̃ sulcat hostiis
Arelatus illic ciuitas attollitur
Theline uocata sub priore sæculo
Graio incolente multa nos rhodano super
Narrare longo res subegerunt stilo
At nunq̃ in illud animus inclinabitur
Europam ut isto flumine & libyam adseram
Disterminari phileus hoc quáquá uetus
Putasse dicat incolas despectui
Derisuiq̃ inscitia hæc sit barbara
Et compete
Cursus carninæ biduo & binoctio est
Gens hinc nearchi bergineq̃ ciuitas
Salyes atroces oppidum priscum ramastrabalæ
Paludes terga celsum prominens
Quod incolentes cecylistrium uocant
Massilia & ipsa est cuius urbis hic situs
Pro fonte littus præiacet tenuis uia
Pater inter undas latera gurges adluit
Stagnum lambit urbem & unda lambit oppidum
Laremq̃ fusa ciuitas pene insula est
Sic æquor omne cæspiti infundit manus
Laboi & olim conditorum diligens
Formam locorum & arua naturalia
Euicit a te si quæ prisca te iuuant
Hæc in nouela nominum deducere

RVFI FFSTIAVIENII OPERA FINIVNT

Editio princeps: 678-714